Ron Mangus

RON MANGUS' CUSTOM HOT ROD INTERIORS SERIES

CHEVY TRI-FIVE
CUSTOM INTERIORS
1955 • 1956 • 1957

RON MANGUS

AND

GARY D. SMITH

California Bill's
Automotive Handbooks

Publishers
Howard W. Fisher
Helen V. Fisher

Editor
Howard W. Fisher

Cover and Interior Design
Gary D. Smith, Performance Design
www.performancedesign.net

Cover and Interior Photography
Gary D. Smith, Performance Design

Published by
California Bill's Automotive Handbooks
P.O. Box 91858
Tucson, AZ 85752-1858
520-547-2462
www.californiabills.com

Distributed to bookstores by
Motorbooks International
729 Prospect Avenue
P.O. Box 1
Osceola, WI 54020-0001

ISBN-10 1-931128-25-1
ISBN-13 978-1-931128-25-4

Printed in China

1 2 3 4 5 6 7 8 9 14 13 12 11 10 09 08

Contents

The Cars

ABOUT THE AUTHORS

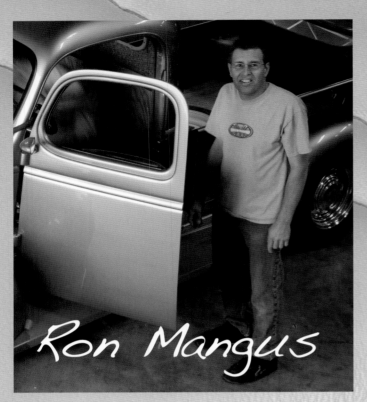

Ron Mangus

Ron started his stitching career in 1969 under the tutelage of his brother Ernie Yanez. Ernie provided special efforts over the course of twenty years in getting Ron started on the right track. Ron credits his brother for teaching him the auto upholstery craft and business, and providing a foundation for the reputation he enjoys today.

In 1989 Ron opened his own shop, Custom Auto Interiors, in Bloomington, California. During this era he also taught basic and advanced upholstery classes at San Bernardino Valley College for four years. Students who were talented enough to take his advanced course learned Ron's techniques for sculpting foam, creating molded headliners, and building custom door panels.

Soon after opening his own shop, a roadster with his interior won America's Most Beautiful Roadster at the 1992 Oakland Roadster Show. Ron's work has since received numerous Best Interior Awards at a variety of car shows.

Ron "The Stitcher" has become famous as a creator of fabulous interiors. From the 1990s through today street rod and hot rodding magazines have featured spectacular cars that show off his interiors.

Photo by Daniel B. Smith

Gary D. Smith

The Riverside International Raceway in Riverside, California, is now a shopping center. But when Gary was a teenager, it was one of the premier road racing tracks in the country. When the Can-Am and Trans-Am came to town, Gary could be found at the Raceway, taking photos. Interest in cars lead to modifying his own street cars and local club drag racing. He crewed on a SCCA Trans-Am Corvette in the mid '70s.

Gary was also interested in car design. He competed in the General Motor's Fisher Body Craftsman's Guild model car design contest, and in 1969 enrolled at the Art Center College of Design in Los Angeles, California. After graduating in 1973 with a degree in Industrial/Transportation design, he was recruited by General Motors Design Staff at the General Motors Technical Center in Warren, Michigan. He worked there as a Senior Creative Designer in Pontiac, Buick, Oldsmobile, and Cadillac exterior design studios. He is responsible for the exterior styling of the Oldsmobile Concept car that lead to the 1992 Oldsmobile Achieva SCX coupe.

In 1988, Gary and his family moved to Arizona, and Gary started Performance Design, freelancing as an industrial/graphic designer and illustrator. Gary also became proficient in desktop publishing and computer graphics. He has been involved with many businesses as an art-director level designer and consultant. In 1996, Gary was introduced to "California Bill" Fisher. Through the relationship that has continued with Bill's son Howard, Gary has been involved in the creation of many automotive titles published by California Bill's Automotive Handbooks.

How-to articles and finished car features showing Mangus' techniques and expertise have appeared in *Hot Rod, Rod & Custom, Street Rodder, Truckin', American Rodder, The Rodder's Journal*, and many more. Special cars with interiors created by Ron and his team include CheZoom and Aluma-Coupe of Boyd's Hot Rods, Billy "ZZ Top" Gibbons' Kopperhed, along with cars for Tim Allen, Pete Chapouris of SO-CAL Speed Shop, Linda Vaughn (Miss Hurst), Thom Taylor, Bruce Meyer, Kenny Bernstein, Robby Gordon, Sammy Hagar, Michael Anthony, Cory McClenathan, and James Brubaker of Universal Studios.

In 2000 Ron was asked to help create a special car for builder Randy Clark from Hot Rods and Custom Stuff of Escondido, California. Their 1949 Chevy Business Coupe won the coveted Ridler award at the Detroit Autorama in 2001. This car was featured on the cover of *Super Rod* in April/May, 2001. This car also won the prestigious "Yosemite" Sam Radoff Sculptural Excellence Award that recognizes both the interior and the entire concept of a car. Ron felt a great accomplishment in achieving these awards.

The 2005 Grand National Roadster Show Best Interior Award went to a 1968 Camaro convertible again upholstered by Ron and built by Randy Clark of Hot Rods and Custom Stuff.

Ron's striking two-tone interior was featured in Richard Tapia's '70 Chevelle winning the 2006 Houston AutoRama's Best of Show as well as Best Interior. This car also won Best of Show at Super Chevy in Pomona, and numerous top awards at the Grand National Roadster Show.

Eventually hot rodders knew Ron's work and reputation by name. So, in 2006, the original shop, Custom Auto Interiors, was renamed Ron Mangus Hot Rod Interiors.

Recently the 2008 Grand National Roadster Best Interior Award went to Ron's creation of Janice Groesbeck's 1956 Chevy convertible.

While Ron is at the highest levels of automotive design and creation, his best work may be yet to come.

INTRODUCTION

I hope you will find my passion and love for these cars in the photographs throughout the book.

What drives my passion? Where do I get the inspiration and vision for each project? Those questions have been asked of me a lot more frequently than you might imagine.

What people tell me is that when a car arrives here, I look at the car and learn about the person who owns the car and try to individualize it to his or her needs and ideas. As a result, every interior ends up with a unique design. I take each car under my wing and treat it like it's my own car and, unfortunately,

I have to give it back when I'm done. I show that passion to my customers, and they sense that when they come in. They feel welcome and, when the job is complete, they know that I have given them the best job with the highest craftsmanship possible.

As you are looking through the photos in this book you will find that, although there may be similarities in approach, each car is completed with its own special characteristics.

Ron Mangus

Ron's Shop

Ron Mangus Custom Hot Rod Interiors is a fast-paced business with tight deadlines. In spite of the rush, Ron pays attention to every detail, with no compromises when it comes to quality, craftsmanship, and design. His hand-picked, dedicated team works together seamlessly, creating the many subassemblies that make up a car's interior. He involves his customers in the design process, discussing the design, material selection, and helps them visualize his ideas on how to blend his customer's desires with the car's character to create a masterpiece.

1
Last minute details are addressed as a 1955 Chevy Bel Air is completed.

2
Ron's son, Ryan, is an important part of the business, and is fast becoming a rising interior design star in his own right.

3
A great friend, Pete Salas has worked with Ron for more than 25 years.

4
Ron is proud of his team for their dedication to quality and craftsmanship. They share Ron's design philosophy, treating every car as if it was their own.

Ron's personal attention to his customers builds long-term relationships, referrals, and repeat business. His "hands-on" involvement with every aspect of the design ensures originality and quality.

Ron's Hot Rods

1

"This '56 Ford pickup was my daily driver for 15 years. It's been in the family since it was purchased new and my son Ryan now has it. It was originally used on my father-in-law's chicken ranch."

2

"My '37 Ford Tudor Sedan broke new ground with a two-tone interior that matched the exterior. It was featured in the *American Rodder Collector Special Edition*, September 1996."

3

"I built this '32 from a Total Cost Involved chassis in 1997. It was painted in gelcoat so I could really enjoy driving the car. I could do a burn out and just plow through puddles. This was my rat rod before they reached their current popularity. It was a great car."

4

"I think I was the first to do a flame billet steering wheel. I should have patented the design!"

5

Ron's T-Roadster, taken in 1988. "The car was fast. It would shift out of low at 65 mph. I had to drive slowly over bumps and approach driveways at an angle because the oil plug was really low, and I didn't want to knock it off. The whole family would crowd into the car to go to cruise night. Ryan and I got caught in the rain more than once. We had a lot of fun with that car."

6

"Having always had a passion for motorcycles I began riding again about eight years ago. Being childhood friends with award winning motorcycle builder Jerry Covington (Covington's Cycle City, Woodward, Oklahoma) allowed me to use one of his rolling chassis. Another friend Dean Padie built this bike."

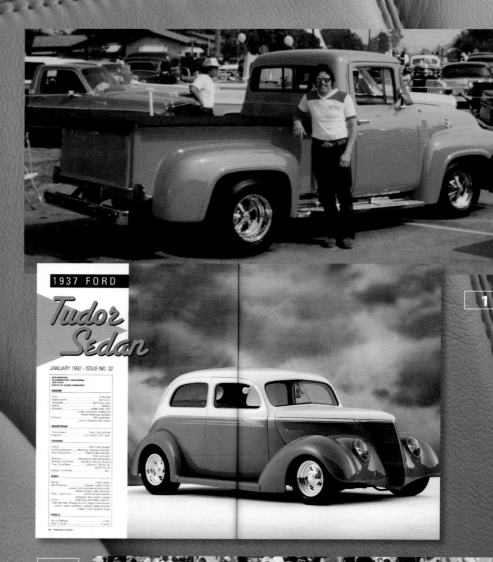

4

5

6

Hot Rodding History

1

This '32 Ford roadster was originally built in 1978 by Barry Lobeck. The 1994 restoration was upholstered by Ron Mangus. *Street Rodder* magazine, March 1995. The Bruce Meyer Collection.

2

Bob Rosenthal's 1936 Ford was first place winner in the 1935–1948 Custom Rod Roadster class at the 2007 Grand National Roadster Show with Ron's interior. *The Rodder's Journal* #34.

3

The "M-80," a '49 Chevy Business Coupe owned by Chris Williams won the Ridler Award in 2001 with upholstery by Ron Mangus. *Super Rod*, April 2001.

4

In the early '60s Dick Bergren made this classic '50s hot rod into one of the most admired and well-proportioned, chopped three window coupes ever. Known as the Doyle Gammell Coupe, it was featured in *Rod and Custom* magazine, December 1963. Bruce Meyer owns the car, and Ron restored the interior to original. *The Rodder's Journal* #29.

5

SO-CAL's Alex Xydias, founder of SO-CAL Speed Shop, came to Ron to upholster the seat for the restored Belly Tank racer that ran 198 mph at Bonneville in 1952. Ron also upholstered the traditional interior for the SO-CAL '32 Hi-boy that started a revolution in hot rodding in the '90s.

6

Here is an integral part of hot rodding history. This is the original chopped top Merc by Sam Barris. This car was recently restored by Roy Brizio Street Rods and is owned by John Mumford. Ron felt honored to help complete this period-correct restoration. *The Rodder's Journal* #38.

4

5

THE BRUCE MEYER COLLECTION

SO-CAL

STOP

SO-CAL

RON-
THANKS FOR YOUR
HELP ON THE TANK!!
Alex Xydias

6

Ron's Customers

1

Tim Allen's 1946 Ford, from the TV show Tool Time. The Ford features distressed leather in '40s–'50s style by Ron Mangus. *Rod & Custom* magazine, April 1999.

2

Jeremy McGrath, the original extreme athlete, made motor sports history with his high-flying freestyle motocross antics. A hot rodder at heart, he went to Ron Mangus to have his '33 Ford upholstered. Built by Dominator Motor Sport Fabrication, Brentwood, California, it won Most Elegant Rod at the inaugural Oakland Rod, Custom, and Motorcycle Show in 2001. *Street Rodder* magazine, September 2003.

3

A 1950 Ford business coupe one-off show car? Ford never made one. Enter Billy "ZZ Top" Gibbons who envisioned the transformation and Pete Chapouris who made it happen. Ron Mangus duplicated the 2-inch Tijuana-style tuck 'n roll from 20-year-old copper vinyl surrounded by bright white. *Hot Rod* magazine, January 1996.

4

Bob Stewart, son of hot rod hero Ed "Axle" Stewart, owns this 1932 Ford. This roadster was built in the 1940s and saw quite a bit of dry lakes action from 1947–1949 and clocked a speed of 128.93 mph on July 18, 1948 at El Mirage. Period interior by Ron Mangus.

5

Rock star singer Sammy Hagar with his buggy in Cabo. Interior by Ron Mangus.

6

Larry Erickson's Aluma-Coupe, built by Boyd Coddington, gave Ron a chance to work with the talented team at Boyd's Hot Rod Shop. This interior was completed without using a single stitch. The sculpted interior was all molded and carefully glued in place.

3

Kopperhed is powered by an overhead—like a .030-inch-over '57 Y-block cooled by a U.S. Radiator, fitted with a three-pot Offy intake sporting Ford carbs, repop air cleaners and detailed cast finned-aluminum rocker covers. F-600 truck exhaust manifolds were ground smooth and sprayed with a high-temp coating.

PC3g wheels—actually 16-inch '49 Ford centers offset-welded by Pete Eastwood to custom-rolled 16x7 rims—support four BFGoodrich P205/55ZR16 radials augmented by Coker-supplied Atlas add-on whitewalls. Presto, radial whites.

KOPPERHED

By Gray Baskerville

Let's pretend that 45 years ago Ford commissioned an artist/designer, such as Steve Stanford, to draw a one-off concept car based on a '50 Ford single-bench-seat business coupe. Let's fast-forward to 1956, when the concept coupe, a three-window precursor to the '55 T-bird, has outlived its usefulness and been sold to a second owner. Luck would have it that the new owner was your middle-of-the-road hot rodder—too lean to do a full custom but fat enough to afford an engine swap and a few other low-buck mods, such as heated front coils, a pair of 4-inch lowering blocks, twin pipes, add-on whites and a "Tijuana" trim job.

That is what Billy "ZZ Top" Gibbons envisioned when he commissioned Pete Chapouris' PC3g (aka re-Pete & Jake's) to create what he calls "Kopperhed." As with many similar rod-related projects that went from hibernation to hypersonic, Kopperhed began as a practical daily-driver upgrade—after Billy had bought an Uncle Daniel one-owner '50 from one of Chapouris and Bob Bauder's clients. Then it soon took on a life of its own—a twist here, a turn there as Reverend Billy's imaginative inclinations ultimately transformed this mundane business coupe into

Photography: Jim Brown/PPC Photographic & Gray Baskerville

Chrome rear-fender beads were a stock option that had to be straightened by Jim "Jake" Jacobs. The only alteration to the stock rear bumper was the removal of the guards.

Ronnie Mangus (and crew) duplicated the 2-inch Tijuana-style seats and door panels with bright white vinyl. The copper insert was made from original 20-year-old material that was obtained from S&S in Oregon. The balance of K-hed's interior elements include custom-shaped, engine-turned step plates, a J.B. Donaldson-restored Crest Liner steering wheel, a Jake-modified dash (to accept the stereo tuner) and a T-Bird-shaped frame. The instruments are original, but the knobs were made by PC3g.

4

6

5

FRED CHAVEZ'S

'57 Chevy Bel Air

When Fred was 16 years old, he heard about a job opening at a local gas station. He hustled over and got the job, and on his first day, into the station rolled a coral 14-year-old Bel Air hardtop equipped with a six-cylinder engine and Powerglide transmission. Fred was taken with it and asked the owner if she'd like to sell it. The owner did need to sell the '57 within two weeks, but she had to have $150. That was a lot in 1971, but Fred came up with the money and has had the car ever since. Fred says that he used to pick up his kids in this car, which was in primer for many years, and has had several engines. Then five years ago his wife, Sylvia, declared "it's time to restore the car." It was competed in April 2008.

The Bel Air's frame is interesting. 1957 Chevrolets came with two kinds of boxed frames in several configurations. According to John Chambers Vintage Chevrolet of Phoenix, Arizona, ninety percent were seamed from two "C" channels. The rest were probably supplied by A.O. Smith, and were made from seamless rectangular section steel. They were called "California frames" and popular in Jr. Stock drag racing in the '60s and '70s because they were believed to be lighter. They should be called "Flint frames" because most seamless frames were used on cars assembled in Flint, Michigan. Fred's car was built in Los Angeles, so it is unusual for a car built in California to have the seamless frame. What kind of frame was used was strictly a matter of supplier availability. It is, however, a nice frame to build a resto-mod, because it has a much smoother appearance than a seamed frame.

Build and Paint: Bryan's Custom Restorations, Fullerton, California
Engine: Corvette LS1
Drivetrain: 4L65E transmission, Corvette C4 IRS
Chassis: Modified stock
Wheels: Pro Wheels Boost: front: 18", rear: 20"

This clean, updated custom version of the original interior isn't overpowering. The design flows with colors and contours, and gives the impression that it's the way it should have come in the first place. Fred had a great experience with Ron who grasped immediately what Fred was after, and thoroughly updated the interior keeping some styling clues from the 1957 Chevrolet design, yet transforming it with modern materials, refining it in terms of comfort and convenience in the process.

Seat springs were pulled down and tightened resulting in lower stock seats. The stainless steel trim on the doors is stock.

1

2

3

1
Plush rear seat features individual seating areas.

2
The carpet on the lower door is continued on the kick panel, and follows the contour of the floor. It adds great detail, and also protects the lower door panel from scuffing.

3
Sculpted ultrasuede® headliner has recessed pockets for sun visors.

4
Rear quarter panels use the stock stainless steel trim. Custom armrests that follow the shape of the stock trim were added for styling and comfort. The power window switch is in its original position in the armrest.

5
German square-weave carpet is used throughout. The air conditioning ducting is hidden behind the leather wrapped custom lower instrument panel extension. It looks great.

1

The interior has an inviting stock look. Ron used both smooth and perforated leathers as well as contrasting inserts on the door panels, quarter panels, and seat backs.

2

Door panels have an elegant simplicity. The sculpted armrests and flush speaker grilles help define the interior as being truly contemporary in every respect, but the stock stainless trim hints back to the '50s.

3

The rear seat side bolster is notched to flow around the sculpted armrest.

4

The classic '57 Chevrolet instrument panel with modern concessions given to instrumentation and the cut-down steering wheel look great.

5

Pleated map pocket adds storage convenience for the driver and passenger.

6–7

The theme from the interior carries into the understated trunk with sculpted design lines picking up the door panel and seat design.

8

The deck lid is covered in ultrasuede®, and has the wide sections to match the headliner.

1

5

6

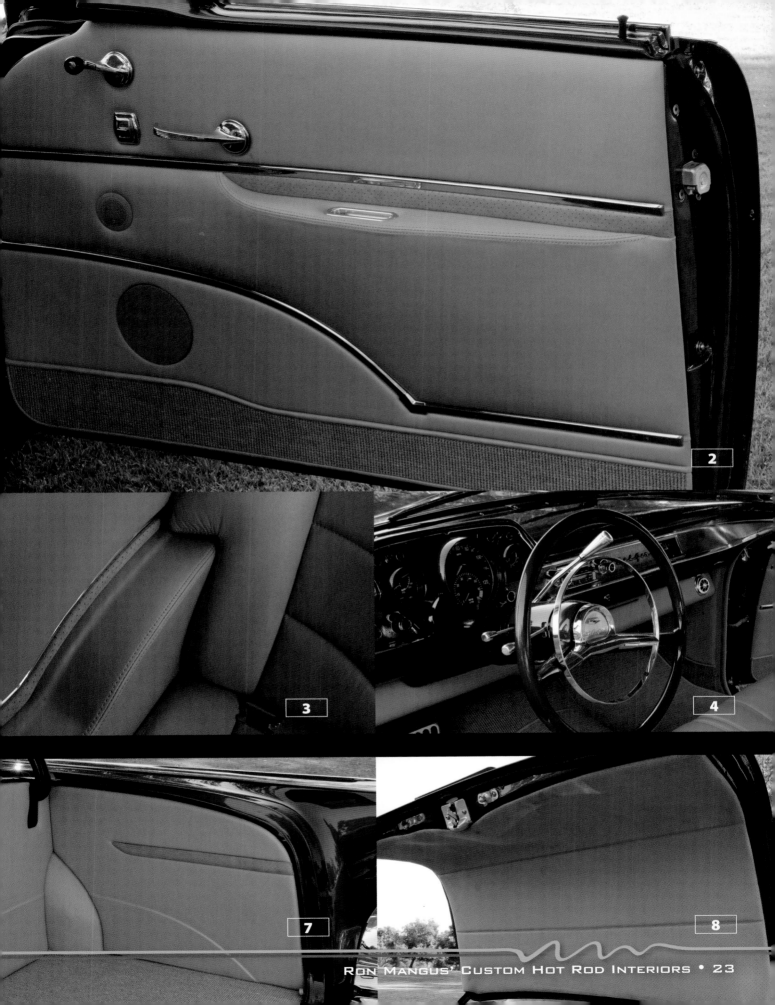

2

3

4

7

8

LENN PRITCHARD'S
'57 Chevy Bel Air Convertible

Lenn found this car in Camp Verde, Arizona. It was equipped with the original fuel-injected engine, and being a convertible, was a rare car in great condition. Sometime after he bought the car, it was extensively damaged by an engine fire. Lenn decided to dramatically upgrade the car mechanically and cosmetically while he was restoring it. The car took six months to finish, and was completed in mid-2004.

The story of the upholstery is equally interesting. Lenn discovered for sale two bolts of the original NOS vinyl upholstery that had been stored in an attic since 1962 by a man who bought the material intending to restore his own car. The car had long since been sold, the attic eventually cleared, and the material ended up on eBay.

With its complete 1990 ZR1 drivetrain, suspension, 6-speed manual transmission, and Paul Newman chassis, the car is fast and fun to drive. Its updated underpinnings are disguised by its stock exterior and orange and silver retro interior.

Ron had a lot of fun with this project. It brought back memories of old-school techniques and use of original vinyl materials. While the original interior design was modified, it still retains most of the original styling clues. 1950s all the way!

Build and Paint: Pioneer Auto, Prescott, Arizona
Engine: Corvette ZR1
Drivetrain: 6-speed manual transmission, Corvette rear end
Chassis: Paul Newman with Corvette ZR1 suspension
Wheels: Budnik

"This was a really fun project that brought back memories of old school techniques and use of materials. I was really pleased with the finished project."—*Ron Mangus*

Lenn had come across NOS fabrics with stock patterns that were used to create an interior very reminiscent of the original Chevrolet design. The finished interior showcases many period correct details.

1

The use of the original upholstery materials and bright colors presents '50s styling at its best. The orange vinyl has horizontal lines in the fabric, and the silver vinyl has small raised circles in the pattern, both adding a great deal of interesting and period correct material texture.

2

The original stainless steel moldings divide the contrasting colors and add a great deal of visual interest.

3

Ron used French stitching for added subtle detail to the armrests. Notice the carefully controlled curves and forms.

4

Power window switches, door and window handles are stock.

5

What's not to like about '57 Chevy authenticity?

2

3

1

4

5

1

The notch in the front bench seat allows space for shifting for the Corvette 6-speed transmission.

2–4

OEM vinyls combined with Ron's sensitivity to the original Chevrolet styling preserves the nostalgic look of 1957. It would be difficult to determine, without direct comparison with a stock '57 Chevy convertible, what the subtle differences are in this car's interior styling.

5

Ron left the power window switch in the original position in the rear armrest.

6–7

Instrument panel is original.

8

The trunk was finished using very basic design and materials that maintain the vintage feel of the car.

1

5

6

2

3

4

7

8

DARWIN GROESBECK'S

'56 Chevy Bel Air

Darwin's "Double Huffer" Bel Air custom show car makes an extreme statement everywhere you look, starting with the engine. The term "scary fast" comes to mind.

The car's flawless black paint is engulfed with wild orange flames. The styling has been customized with interesting touches including a '54 Chevy grille, a roof vent from a '58 Chevy turned into a third brake light, and smoothed drip rails. The car has been nosed, decked, and the stock three-piece bumper shortened, welded, reshaped, and installed upside down.

The car was originally purchased as a donor parts car for his wife's '56 Chevy convertible, but they decided to resto-mod the Bel Air hardtop instead of using it for parts. The car was completed in 2005.

Ron's interior is also extreme, with lots of polished stainless steel and billet aluminum trim, black and gray leather custom seating, and black anodized aluminum flame trim recessed into the seat backs. The tapered, windswept shapes of the interior design elements speak volumes about the unrestrained nature of the entire car.

The car has won numerous awards, and has been featured in several national magazines.

Build and Paint: Extreme Automotive, Corona, California
Engine: Chevy 502/502, two Paxton Superchargers, Nitrous
Drivetrain: GM 4L80E transmission, Ford 9-inch rear end
Chassis: Jim Meyer Racing Products, Lincoln City, Oregon
Wheels: Boyd Coddington Smoothie II, front: 17", rear: 18"
Tires: Nitto

The dark interior makes for quite a dramatic backdrop for the wildly shaped polished stainless steel trim. Black anodized aluminum flames recessed into the seat backs are another reminder of the unrestrained personality of the car.

Nothing in the interior has escaped interesting form transitions. Notice the lower instrument panel blending into the console, the shape surrounding the array of seat controls on the shifter console, and the cascading waterfall rear armrest.

1
There is a lot going on in the rear passenger area, with the center armrest resting in a curve on the console. The center armrest also sweeps up into the package shelf and meets the quarter panel armrest in a curved shape that encompasses the speaker grilles.

2
The quarter panel armrest's double dip parallels the quarter window sill shape. Wild stuff.

3
Flames recessed into the center of the seat backs are water jet cut aluminum, then black powder coated.

4
Notice how the lower instrument panel blends into the top of the console. The side of the console has a great deal of form and interest. The center stack has sound system and climate controls.

5
The front of the sculpted headliner has recessed pockets for the sun visors, and also features a mini roof console from a late model Suburban with map lights and storage.

4

5

2

Ron designed the bright hard trim door panel pieces to incorporate the door release. These parts were water jet cut from stainless steel.

3

Uniquely shaped polished stainless steel shifter console plate provides a convenient place for seating and window controls.

4

The lower instrument panel flows seamlessly into the console.

5

The trunk is no less entertaining than the interior, with its curved alcove and resident polished chrome nitrous tank. The underside of the deck lid repeats the contrasting gray sculpted insert headliner design.

6

Close-up of the curved intersection of the center armrest and console.

7

Darwin's Chevy showcases custom polished stainless steel and billet aluminum trim.

8

The attention to detail is what sets Ron's interiors apart.

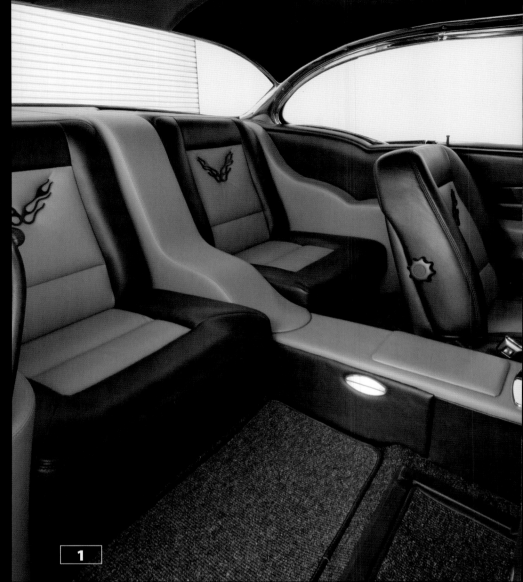

1

5

6

2

4

7

8

BERT ROBERTS'
'55 Chevy Bel Air

After searching four states looking for a Bel Air hardtop, Bert found this car five miles from home at the Pomona swap meet. Not surprisingly, when the paint was stripped from the body, the car turned out to have looked better than it actually was. That may be, but it's laser straight now. Bert took three years to build the car, and it was completed in August 2007.

Bert's desire was to have the best of both worlds—a classic stock-appearing '55 that sat well on its wheels, with hot rod power and exhaust sound, reminding him of rods he used to own. This re-creation benefits from 52 years of automotive technology, and combines a thoroughly modern drivetrain, chassis, and upgraded creature comforts into a package that rivals the best of what is available anywhere today.

Bert enjoyed the design experience working with Ron to develop the interior. Bert had interior renderings created, and as the design process developed, the concept matured into a masterful blend of thoroughly up-to-date materials and comfort with touches of '50s retro by creating custom chrome-plated brass trim. The "hard look" sculpted seating and door panel design is repeated in the leather headliner panels which are reminders of headliner bows typical of the period. The results speak for themselves.

Built by: Bert Roberts
Paint: Hung Lu Custom Painting, Azusa, California
Engine: 2004 Chevy 5.3 liter, intercooled Magnacharger
Drivetrain: GM 4L60E, Ford 9-inch rear end
Chassis: Modified stock by Williams Classic Chassis,
    La Verne, California
Computer and Electrical: Eclipse Engineering, Whittier, California
Wheels: Budnik Muroc II, front: 7"×17", rear: 9.5"×17"
Tires: Toyo, front: 215/50×17", rear: 225/60×17"

The inlaid chrome door moldings hint at this '55 Bel Air's roots, yet add contemporary style and luxury to the interior.

The original '55 Chevy had stainless steel door panel trim. New technology allows Ron to repeat the custom look by using chrome plated brass trim that is fabricated by Louie Check of Red Lizard Moulding, San Bernardino, California.

1
The contour of the hand formed rear bench seat was shaped to match the cut down Lexus front seats.

2
Careful consideration was given to the owner's driving comfort of this '55. For example, the center console and door panel armrests were carefully designed at the same height.

3
An iPod dock and cup holders are built in. The padded module resting on the front of the console conceals the sound system controls.

4
Ron fabricated custom floor mats from German square-weave carpet and included a matching leather heal pad.

5
Speaker grilles shapes were patterned from the rear-view mirrors. The owner played an integral role in the design of his interior, offering considerable input in its development.

2

3

1

4

5

1

There is considerable styling restraint and craftsmanship that contributes to the high-end look. The paneled headliner looks like bows typical of the era, and the grooves between the panels pick up the seat theme.

2

This interior has a fresh, contemporary look, yet retains many design elements and clues that suggest its '50s heritage. The diagonal pattern in between the door trim carries the theme of the seat inserts.

3

Custom designed chrome door panel trim is carried into the rear quarters of the interior.

4

This upholstery style is called the "hard look." Ron uses a specific foam density with a lot of experience to produce these carefully crafted results.

5–7

The interior theme is carried into the trunk of the '55 using matching leather and German square-weave carpet.

8

Sun visors are recessed into pockets in the sculpted leather headliner.

1

5

6

BOB BRKICH'S
'55 Chevy Nomad

Bob's Nomad belonged to a farm owner in Sacramento, California. The car eventually went up for sale in Arizona, and a friend of Bob's told him about it. The car was in excellent original condition, and ran fine.

Bob and a few of his buddies put the car together, extensively reworking the car. It was seamed and filled, straightened, all of the glass replaced, and all of the bright trim polished, re-chromed, or replaced. The stance is accomplished with Air Ride ShockWave air suspension on the front with 2" dropped spindles, and reworked rear springs with 2" lowering blocks. The car took one year to build, and was finished in July 2006.

The interior is trimmed in light tan gloveskin leather with boarskin inserts. Ron incorporated many custom convenience features in the interior. The design is restrained, fluid, and keeps many of the styling elements from the original factory design. Theme continuity is accomplished by repeating trim materials and sculptured lines from front door panels through to the rear quarter panels.

Built by: Bob Brkich
Paint: Tony's Auto Body, Corona, California
Engine: Chevy Ramjet 350 with MEFI IV injection
Drivetrain: GM 700 R4, NOS 1955 Chevrolet 3:55 Positraction
    rear end
Chassis: Modified stock, Air Ride ShockWave air suspension and
    2" dropped spindles in front, reworked rear springs and
    2" lowering blocks
Wheels: Boze Doons, front: 16", rear: 17"

Bob's Nomad has a striking stance on the outside, and a mild custom interior on the inside with two-tone leather, and many custom styling touches and comfort upgrades. The steering wheel was cut down from 17" to 15" by J. B. Donaldson in Phoenix, Arizona, then leather wrapped.

The stock headliner bows and dome lights were kept original. Ron reworked a Glide Engineering split seat with folding armrest by shortening the top of the seat back to keep it at the same height as the window sills.

1

2

3

1
The styling theme that began on the front door panels is continued on the rear quarter panels. Restyled bench seat folds like the original. The six-disc CD changer is under the back seat on the driver's side. Notice the lighter edging on the carpet and mats.

2
The door design extends into the kick panels.

3
Console form is very fluid and organic, and features built-in cupholders.

4
The console is trimmed like the seat in contrasting leathers with different textures.

5
The shoulder strap take-up spool is mounted low and forward on the rear quarter panel. The front door panel design continues through to the rear quarter panel.

4

5

1
Bob's Nomad's interior is very inviting, and looks comfortable and contemporary.

2
The stock stainless trim was retained, but covered in leather. The covered trim becomes a stripe in the upper section of the door and quarter panels.

3
There is a lot of smooth, compound form development in the armrests.

4
This detail shows clearly the differences in texture of the contrasting leathers.

5
Opening the tailgate shows off the matching rear compartment trim.

6
The rear seat folds down like the original, and the seat back goes around the wheel wells to provide as much rear passenger comfort as possible.

7
Bob kept the stock Bel Air speaker grille and script.

8
Lower instrument panel extension hides air conditioning plumbing, and provides a tidy way to finish off the lower dash.

1

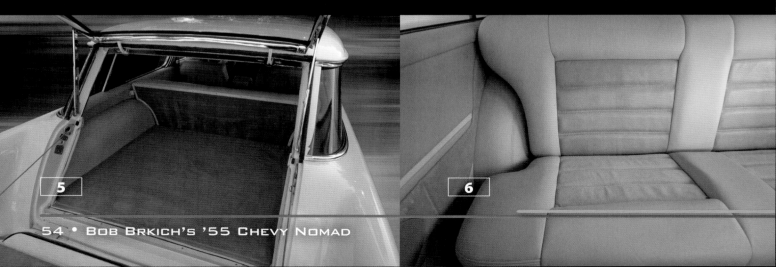

5

6

2

3

4

7

8

GARY BUNKER'S

'56 Chevy Two-Ten

Gary's '56 was found at a Pomona, California swap meet. The sandblasted bare body was intact, but the hood and deck lid had to be replaced and the top extensively reworked because those surfaces had been used as a trampoline more than once. But you'd never know it by looking at it now.

Larry Thomas searched for parts for three years, and needed another year to build the car. Gary talked Larry into selling him the '56, then it went to Ron's shop for the interior work. The car was completed in September 2006.

The idea behind the creation of the car was to build an elegant, yet traditional, hot rod. Ron's interior design certainly conveys the elegance, with his original, sculpted, "hard-look" interior design. The interior is trimmed in camel and cream leather, and uses cut down Lexus front seats.

Ron's attention to detail is evident. The curves in the design of the door panels, seats, trunk, headliner, and console blend together creating a unified, professional look. Cream leather inserts complement the design.

Build and Paint: Larry Thomas, Prescott, Arizona
Engine: 427 Chevy
Drivetrain: GM Turbo 400 Transmission, Ford 9-inch rear end
Chassis: Modified Stock
Wheels: 18" Boyd Coddington Spire custom "one-offs"
Tires: Goodyear Eagles

If it weren't for the instrument panel, you'd be hard pressed to know that this interior is in a car that is more than five decades old.

The profile of the front of the console armrest is repeated in the lines and forms of the door panels, kick panels, and in the seat trim, fully integrating the design.

1

2

3

1
Ron adapted the contours of the Lexus front seats in the custom rear bench. The Lexus front seats are cut down to remove the head rests and provide contemporary comfort and rounded styling that complements the forms of the '56.

2
The center stack conveniently houses the sound system and climate controls.

3
The console form continues on the floor in the rear at the same height as the section under the shifter.

4
The driver enjoys an updated seating position, tilt wheel, comfortable and supportive seating with fully motorized adjustment, and pleasing materials, colors, and textures throughout the entire interior.

5
There are many seemingly insignificant design elements in the interior, but they add up to a quality, well thought out design. For example, the sculpted design line that continues from the door panel into the kick panel intersects the round speaker grille above its center line, resulting in a dynamic, instead of static, relationship between the two styling elements.

1

Ron's door panels have a streamlined look, with highly stylized, windswept forms. The lighter leather insert adds a focal point and accents the design.

2

The lighter accent leather form that began with the front door panels concludes in the sculpted rear armrests. The rear seats feature individual seating areas with ample thigh support and seat side bolsters.

3

Attention to detail is one of the things that sets Ron's interiors apart.

4

The headliner with its sculpted insert is really wild. Not just merely an inlaid panel, it is a very highly styled design element in its own right, and a highlight of the interior.

5–6

The trunk's styling repeats the interior theme, including the light leather insert which also looks like a stylized Chevy "V."

7

The underside of the deck lid has similar detailing found in the headliner.

8

The front of the sculpted headliner inlay resolves itself before getting to the front of the headliner. The recessed sun visor pockets add to the integrated, custom look.

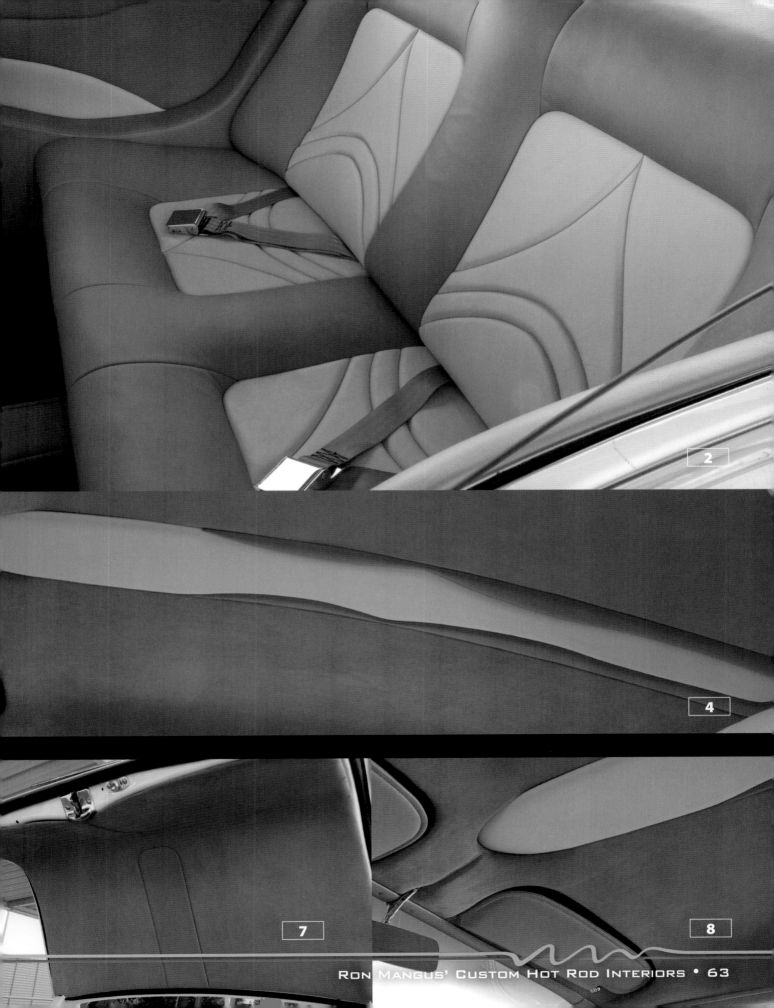

'55 Chevy Bel Air

For Cyndi Testa, 1955 has special significance. She was born that year, and for her 16th birthday was given a 1955 Chevy 2-door just like this one. She drove the car for years. Later, she and her husband Nick decided to restore the '55, only to discover that the car needed more work than they could give it. So the car was sold, and this one was eventually found as a suitable replacement, one with a much better foundation to build on.

Pete Chapouris, street-rod builder and creator of the ZZ Top Eliminator coupe, rents a building owned by Nick, and one day Nick asked Pete if he would take on the project. The car was to maintain a stock appearance, but the chassis and drivetrain modified to modern standards. The result is this stunning azure blue and white Bel Air that looks like it could have rolled off the assembly line—in 1997.

Ron's interior shows considerable design restraint, respecting Cyndi's desire to keep a stock appearance. Yet Ron's contemporary touches update the interior's design and comfort level, and are still consistent with the car's stock look.

One more thing. When Cyndi registered the car in California, she discovered that the car was first registered on her birthday in 1955. It appears that Cyndi and this '55 were meant to be united.

Built by: Pete Chapouris, Pomona, California
Paint: John Carambia, Hemet, California
Engine: High-output 350 Chevrolet crate motor
Drivetrain: Modified stock, Richmond 5-speed
Wheels: 15" American Racing Torq-Thrust II

Cyndi's '55 Bel Air maintains an original stock appearance using upgraded materials. Ron completely reworked the stock seats.

Ron covered the stock seat with white leather. He picked up the curved "V" from the original stainless trim on the door panels and repeated the design on the seat backs.

1

2

3

1
The rear seat may be stock, but Ron added subtle side and center bolsters, and additional padding and thigh support to improve the comfort and appearance of the seat.

2
The white interior looks spacious, inviting, and classic-retro.

3
The stock stainless trim was retained. Ron sculpted a new armrest to update the look of the door panels.

4
Notice the sculpted armrests built into the rear quarter panels.

5
The seats may be less complex than others Ron has designed, but careful attention is still paid to every curve and form. French stitching is used throughout the interior.

4

5

1

The stock front seat was completely rebuilt and recontoured.

2

The door panel design is a nice blend of reusing the stock stainless trim and adding contemporary sculpted armrests. Notice that the lower edge of the armrest shape continues the angled section of the trim, sweeping down and toward the rear.

3

There is always something special about timeless '50s styling.

4

The shifter boot is made from white leather.

5

Stock door handles and window cranks were used in the new interior.

6

Ron pays very close attention to the quality of stitching and the shapes of design lines, whether it is for an exotic custom or an interior that retains a more stock appearance like this one.

7–8

The trunk trim is unique. Cyndi wanted the simple stock look. Ron used the same carpet on the floor and the same trim on the bulkhead that is in the interior.

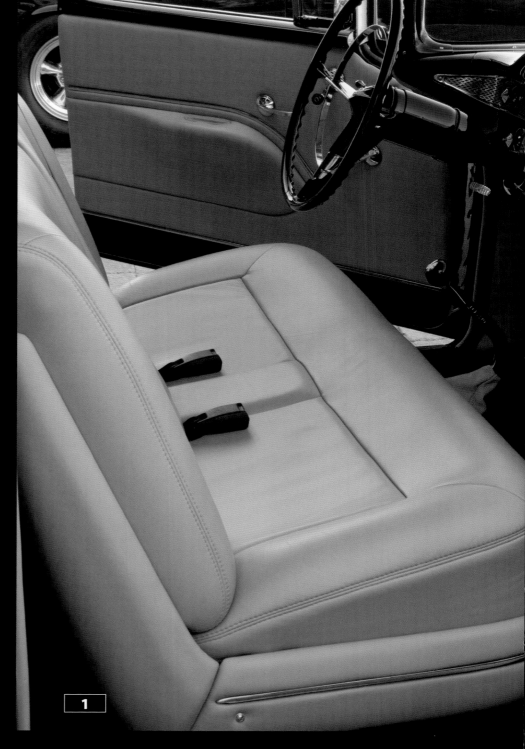

1

5

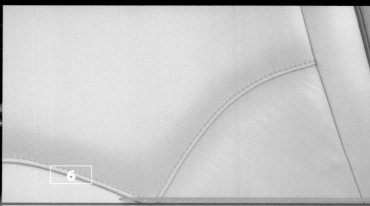

6

2

3

4

7

8

'55 Chevy Nomad

Larry rescued this Nomad from being turned into a drag racer. The front clip had to be replaced as the original was welded together to make a tilt front end. In fact, all of the trim mounting holes and door handles were welded up as well, and the frame had to be replaced. Even though the "top and glass were in great shape," there was a lot of body work to be done to bring the car into the condition you see here. The car was completed in September 2007.

Of the three years Nomads were produced, the 1955 has many more specific sheet metal and custom trim parts than those of the '56 or '57. Parts for a '55 are harder to find and more expensive. After he rounded up the parts he needed, Larry spent about a year of 10-hour days to complete the car.

Ron's sculpted "hard-look" leather interior with pigskin inserts uses Lexus front seats and carries the design into the hand-crafted rear seating area with a flowing console and matching individual rear seats. The fold down rear seat was eliminated in favor of bucket seats.

This outstanding interior is comfortable and functional with close attention paid to every detail.

Build and Paint: Larry Thomas, Prescott, Arizona
Engine: Chevy 400 bored .040" over
Drivetrain: 700R4 transmission, narrowed Ford 9-inch rear end
Chassis: Modified Stock
Wheels: Boyd Coddington New Wave, front: 17", rear: 18"
Tires: BF Goodrich

Larry's Nomad has a clean, integrated, contemporary look. The pigskin accents in the seats, sculpted design lines in the seating areas, and German square-weave carpet all contribute a contrast in texture to the smooth, "hard-look" leather.

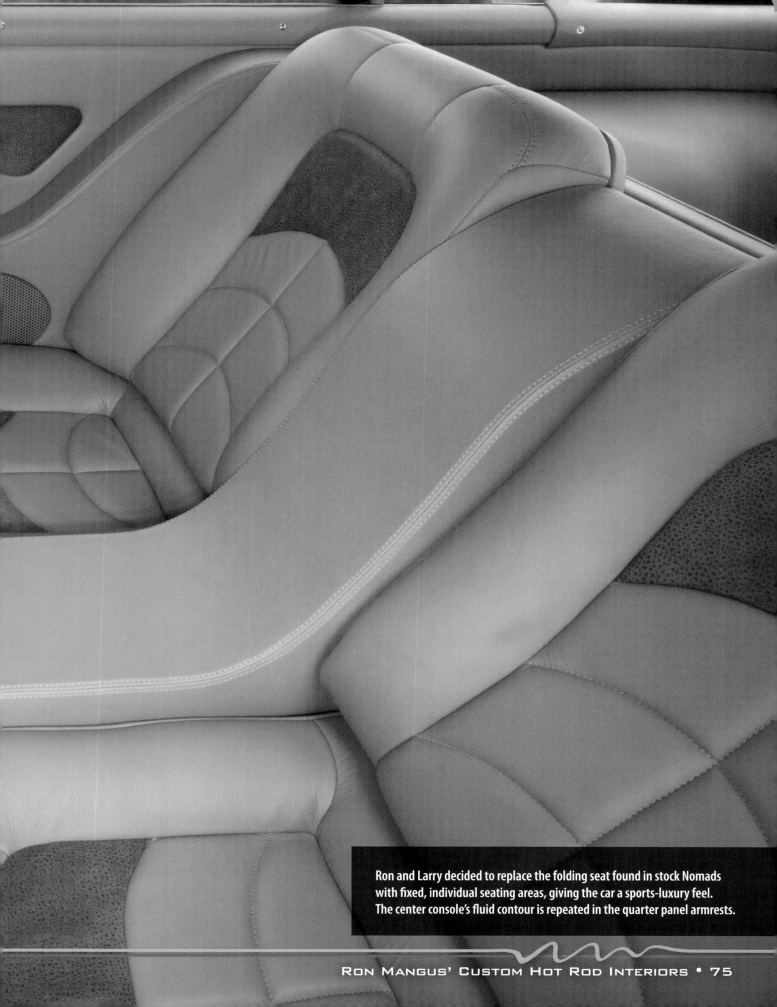

Ron and Larry decided to replace the folding seat found in stock Nomads with fixed, individual seating areas, giving the car a sports-luxury feel. The center console's fluid contour is repeated in the quarter panel armrests.

1

2

3

1
Individual bucket seats contribute to the luxury sports car look and feel of the interior.

2
The inlaid pigskin that starts on the front door panels continues on the rear quarter panels, and concludes with a flare before reaching the upswept armrest.

3
The leather-wrapped console has a smooth, flowing form that spills down from the center armrest.

4
The floor material and mats are nicely tailored from German square-weave carpet.

5
Sound system and climate controls are centrally located in the lower instrument panel and front of the console. All of the shapes blend together in a unified design theme. The kick panels are gently curved, and the large round speaker grilles serve as graphic interest.

4

5

1
The original chrome headliner bows were retained, highlighted by the ultrasuede® leather headliner.

2
A high level of craftsmanship is apparent in the design and control of the sculpted seat inserts. French stitching is used throughout.

3
Recessed sun visor pockets add a contemporary, custom touch to the headliner.

4
The details make the difference. The door handle is installed so that the angle is parallel to the leading edge of the pigskin door panel insert.

5–6
Eliminating the folding back seat provides an additional storage opportunity in the rear compartment. A curved, custom panel conceals the battery and fire extinguisher.

7
The full forms of the back seat storage area and rear quarter covers are nicely shaped and complement forms found in the rest of the interior.

8
The tailgate provided Ron with an additional opportunity to repeat the door panel design at the back of the car, complete with pigskin insert.

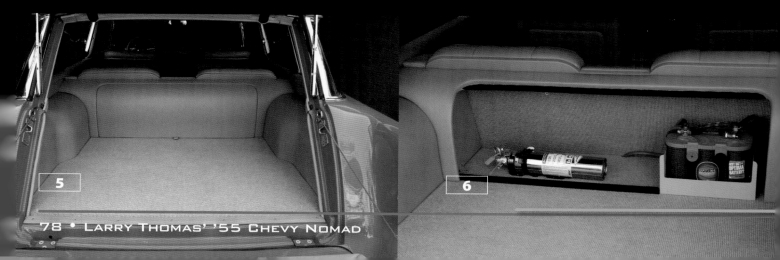

5

6

2

3

4

7

8

IM BURR'S
'57 Chevy Two-Ten

ri-Five Chevys have interesting histories, and this one is no exception. Instead of the usual exhaustive search to find just the right car to begin a project, this '57 found its own way to its new owner. It belonged to a cousin of one of Jim's friends living in Victorville, California. It was used as a drag car in the 1970s, then sat in a carport for 20 years. Jim's friend picked it up from his cousin, and stopped by Jim's house to spend the night on the way to the Pomona swap meet to sell the car. When Jim saw the solid '57 on the trailer, he had to have it.

This is Jim's sixth car that he built himself. He remarks that the car runs great with the LS1, and is very comfortable. It's laser straight with no door dips, and the finish is flawless. The car took two years to build, and was completed in June 2006.

Jim and Ron have been friends since the '80s, and this is the fourth car Ron has upholstered for Jim. The high-end, comfortable feel of the interior is due to the nicely shaped Lexus seats, and the use of blue and parchment leather. The blue breaks up and visually thins the door and quarter panels, and the blue carpet separates the seats and console into design elements. The interior design is not visually complex, but smooth and flowing, and thoroughly contemporary in every respect.

Built by: Jim Burr
Paint: Hot Rods and Custom Stuff, Escondido, California
Engine: Chevy LS1
Drivetrain: GM 4L60E transmission, Ford 9-inch rear end
Chassis: Modified stock
Wheels: 17" Boyd Coddington Stingray
Tires: Dunlop

This isn't Ron's first two-tone interior by any means, but it's one of his best. The use of contrasting leathers breaks up the interior, isolating and visually thinning the groups of design elements.

The interior looks like a pleasant and comfortable place to spend a few traveling hours. Ron used three different kinds of cream leathers. Smooth leather for the bolsters and sides of the seat, perforated leather for seating areas, and matching pigskin for the seat back inserts.

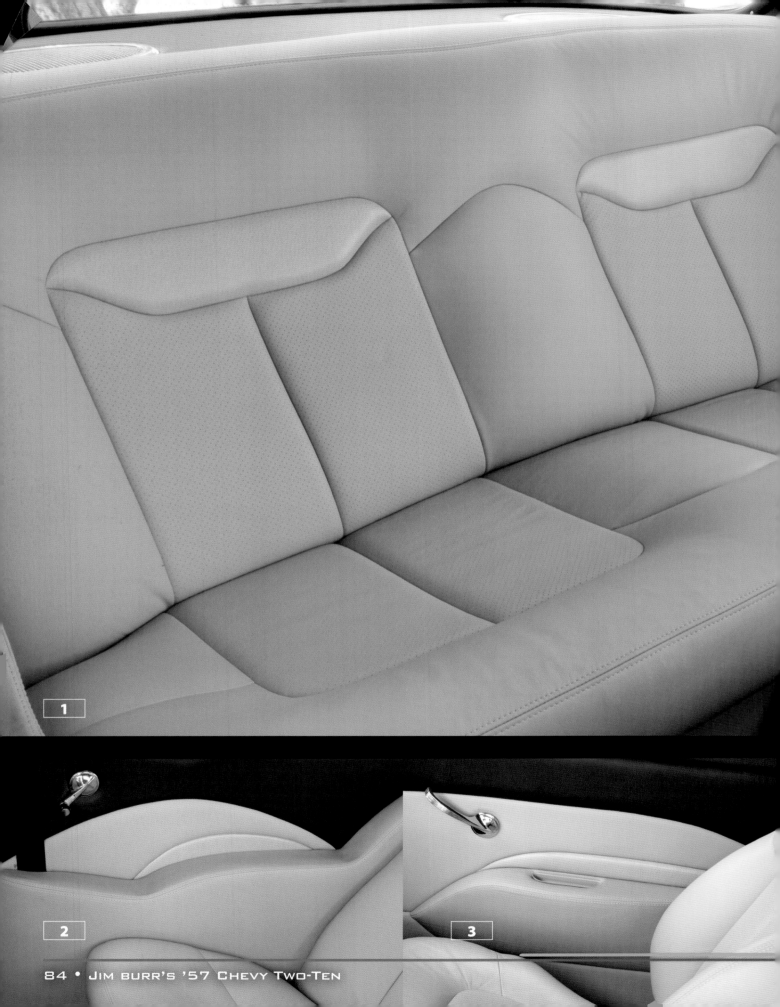

1

2

3

1
Without a central console dividing the rear seat, it looks plush and spacious. Notice that the stitch lines on the seating inserts and the lines on the side and center bolsters are intentionally misaligned. This is for visual interest, as it makes the design dynamic. Misaligning stitch intersections also provides a practical method to resolve fabric fabrication issues.

2
The front seat shoulder strap is spooled up inside the forward portion of the armrest. The rear quarter panels have a very interesting two-tone leather design.

3
All of the sculpted curves and textures on the door panels nicely complement each other.

4
The line separating the blue leather from the rest of the door panel appears to sweep upward from the lower corner of the instrument panel. Notice the sculpted horizontal line that continues into the kick panel.

5
Many design decisions go into every component of an interior. In this photo you can see the relationship between the curves of the front of the console cushion and the corresponding shapes on the seat bolster.

4

5

1

Ron blended textures, curves, and full seat forms into a very graphic and inviting interior.

2

The door panels exhibit a pleasing blend of shapes and curves.

3

Ron wrapped the steering wheel in the same contrasting blue interior leather.

4

The console follows the form development found in the rest of the interior. Built-in cup holders are conveniently placed and graphically break up the top of the console.

5

The mini-console houses speakers, and air conditioning vents and controls.

6

Stock instrument panel with updated gauge cluster keeps most of the original look of the interior intact.

7

Three different leather textures are used in the interior to not only create visual interest, but also to change the way the leathers feel to the touch.

8

Ron makes sure that the French stitching is tight and the sculpted forms are exactly as he envisions.

1

5

6

2

3

4

7

8

DAN BISSELL'S
'57 Chevy Bel Air

Dan developed a passion for '57 Chevys in his high school days. After he and his wife Barbara raised their family, Dan was finally able to fulfill one of his life's ambitions, having his own '57. While looking for a Nomad, he ran across this Bel Air hardtop owned by a body shop owner who faced an ultimatum from his wife of "no more cars." The car was incomplete, but the body was straight.

Dan took a test ride in another car with a Paul Newman chassis, and was blown away by the incredible handling. As a result he bought a chassis with a LS1 engine and six-speed transmission from Newman Car Creations. Dan's '57 took six years to complete and was finished in May 2007.

It has won numerous awards, including the Boyd Coddington's Pro's Pick at the 2007 Goodguys car show in Del Mar, California.

The interior creation process was unique. Dan had Chris Brown of Barry White's Speed Shop create three interior design concepts. Then he and Ron blended the ideas together to create the final design. Dan's brother, Ron, designed the instrument panel featuring a 2005 Ford Five Hundred clock surrounded by burrow walnut.

Ron Mangus cut down the Lexus front seats, and fabricated the rear seats to match. The rich blend of black and tan leather with walnut trim is stunning. The fit and finish is outstanding—truly a world-class interior.

Paint: Black Lazarus by Tony's Restoration
Stainless finished by: Hjeltness Restoration, Escondido, California
Chassis: Newman Car Creations, Paso Robles, California
Drivetrain: Chevy LS1 with 6-speed manual transmission
Engine cover: Designed by Barry's Speed Shop, Corona, California, and
    fabricated by Marcel's Custom Metal Shaping, Corona, California
Exhaust: Barry's Speed Shop, Corona, California
Wheels: 18" Budnik Muroc II • Tires: Nitto-NY 450

The interior features a luxurious three-tone palette that combines rich cinnamon brown and black leather with burrow walnut. The instrument panel and window frames are leather wrapped.

Lexus seats are used in the front with matching individual seating areas in the rear. The dominant console dramatically links the seating areas together.

1

The console extends straight through the interior, splitting the rear seat and creating individual seating areas.

2

The rounded forms of the hand fabricated center armrest repeat the shapes of the front of the console.

3

Shifter location is perfectly positioned, and the power window switches are conveniently located.

4

The burrow walnut accent flows from the front door panel and follows the window and armrest contours.

5

The under-dash panel conceals the air conditioning unit. Note the smooth leather style that continues from the door panel onto the kick panel.

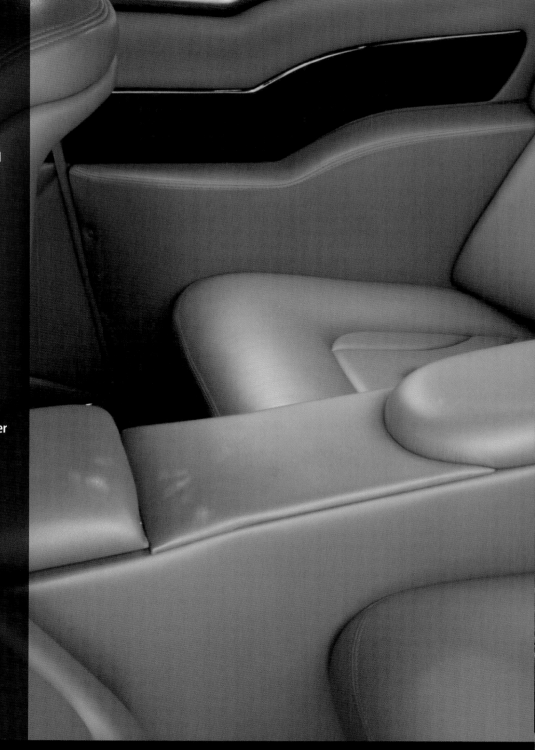

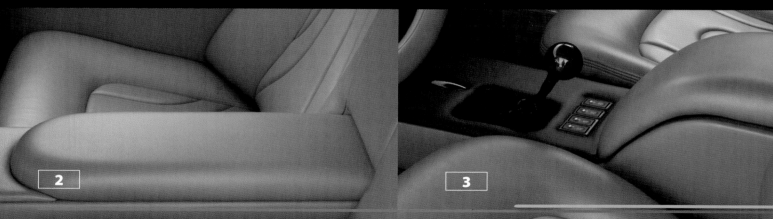

2

3

1

4

5

1
The high-density foam Ron uses allows him to create tight, clean design lines into the leather seat inserts. Notice the carefully controlled curves.

2
The door panels carry the rich tri-tone design through the car. A gracefully formed armrest along with the bright billet door handle completes the design.

3
Ron carefully perforated the leather in a custom pattern and recessed the tweeters in the door panel.

4
The sculpted headliner is all leather, and incorporates stock dome lights.

5–7
The interior theme is continued into the trunk with leather-wrapped panels.

8
Sun visors are recessed into sculpted pockets in the hand formed leather headliner.

1

5

6

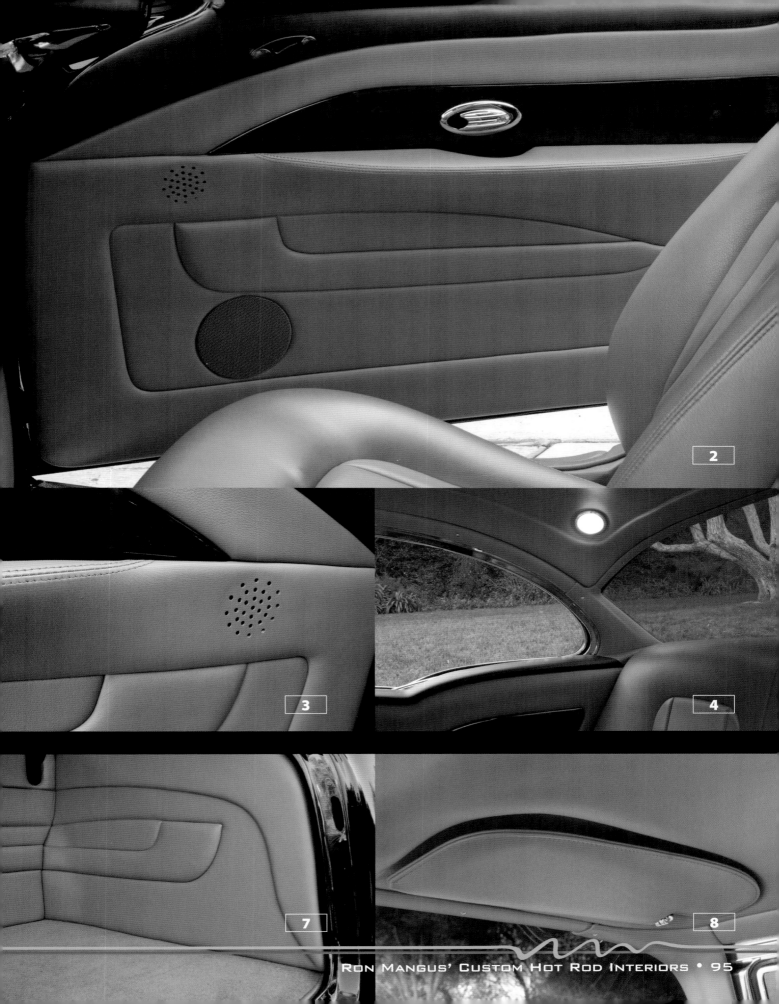

GLEN KANOS'
'55 Chevy Bel Air

Glen's Bel Air has been in his family since 1958. It was set up as a street racer in the late '50s and early '60s before street racing was not so frowned upon. Glen's brother Gregory was the one doing the racing when Glen was a teenager, and one of the favorite drag racing spots was on Imperial Highway in El Segundo. The '55 was eventually put in storage for 30 years, and was in excellent condition when the restoration began. The car took seven years to build, and was completed in November 2006.

The uniquely designed car has a southern California surfboard look and feel, with its bright Torch Red exterior, and light camel leather interior with painted metal trim. The car is built on a hand-crafted chassis, supported by C4 Corvette independent front and rear suspension. There are many hand-made features in the car, including custom steel inner fenders, radiator support, and engine cover.

Ron's interior uses cut down Lexus SC400 front seats, creating the rear seat to match. The red inset panel theme is repeated in the console, door panels, headliner, and trunk. Red stitching complements the organic look and feel of the design. As always, Ron's attention to detail and design continuity is evident as the design theme starts with the front kick panels, and extends through the sculpted door panels and into the rear quarter panels. The interior was completed in a heroic two week effort to make the 2006 SEMA show.

Build and Paint: Bryan's Custom Restoration, Fullerton, California
Engine: Chevy LS1
Drivetrain: 4LE60 transmission
Chassis: Custom fabricated with C4 Corvette suspension
Wheels: 18" Budnik Tiller 5
Tires: Dunlop

The interior features a cream leather interior with painted red metal accents in the headliner, instrument panel, console, door panels, and under the deck lid. It is a very organic design in sculpted leather. Glen lived just a few miles from the beach, so it's not surprising that the interior comes across as a rolling California surf board.

Often a design is too complex to send a finished car to Ron's shop for upholstery, because competed assemblies would have to be taken apart, duplicating work and presenting opportunities to damage finished parts. In this case the console was built by Bryan's Custom Restoration and the incomplete car was shipped to Ron on a dolly. He covered only the instrument panel and center console so those components could be completed by the builder. There has to be a great deal of professional trust and respect between builders to be able to do this.

1
With the seat folded forward for access to the rear seat, the dominating central console is clearly visible. Notice the armrest form flowing from the front door panel to the rear quarter panel.

2
Ron swelled the form of the headliner to create very deep, organic pockets for the sun visors. Also depicted is the way the forward part of the headliner form is resolved, and the subtle depression for the rear view mirror.

3
The forward console is very full and rounded. German square-weave carpet is used for floor covering and for the floor mats.

4
A single sculpted design line carries the front door panel theme into the kick panel.

5
Ron's attention to detail is everywhere. Even though the forward console had to be split for assembly and access to mechanical components, the joint is sculpted and looks intentional.

2

3

1

4

5

1

Ron uses a consistent vocabulary of smooth forms and transitions, as well as consistent shapes and patterns for a unified design.

2

The lower trailing edge of the sculpted area around the hard red insert blends back to the armrest with a subtle curve, repeating the dip in the quarter window.

3

The headliner with its recessed hard red insert takes the theme overhead. The shapes are interesting, and have a surfboard-on-the-roof kind of feel.

4-6

The interior theme is carried into the trunk, including a similar treatment to the underside of the deck lid to that found on the headliner. Notice the additional metal that was added below the weather strip channel, inside the trunk. This additional material provides an opportunity to carefully control the curve and edge of the intersection between the car and interior trim, and enables Ron to fabricate closeout panels that fit much better than if the edge were left stock. This modification must be done at the body fabrication stage of the car's development.

7

Glen's car is very inviting and pleasing, and looks great in the "warm California sun."

2

3

6

7

NICK TESTA'S
'55 Chevy Nomad

Nick spotted this stock Nomad at a car show with a for sale sign that read "39,000." He and everyone else assumed that was the asking price. It wasn't until he looked in the driver's window and noticed that the odometer read 39,000. A dollar a mile? Taking a closer look at the for sale sign read 39,000 *miles*. He talked to the owner, and went home to consider buying the car. The next morning, he got to the show very early to buy the car. After finalizing the purchase, a close friend of his showed up with the same intention. The friend still wants to buy it.

The Nomad was a 95-point car equipped with the original 265 and Powerglide when Nick bought it. But after living with the outdated suspension, brakes, and leaky transmission, he decided it was time make some upgrades. Nick has done frame-on restorations in the past, but was never satisfied with the results. This Nomad was a frame-off resto-mod.

Ron's interior kept many styling elements from the original stock interior with subtle changes. The seats, for example, are trimmed like the original only the colors are reversed. The original stainless trim was also retained. Perforated, pleated leather adds authenticity to the look and feel of the interior. The original chrome headliner bows were also retained.

The car comes across as an original, but the factory never built one like this. A beautiful example of just how far restraint can get you.

Built by: Pete Chapouris, Pomona, California
Paint: John Carambia, Hemet, California
Engine: Chevy 350 Ramjet
Drivetrain: 700 R4, Ford 9-inch rear end
Chassis: Modified stock by Total Cost Involved, Ontario, California
Wheels: 15" American Racing Torq-Thrust II

The original Chevy Nomad interior still shows through the many upgrades and refinements. The seats are trimmed in leather, with the colors reversed from the stock Nomad interior.

Stock chrome headliner bows and stainless trim contribute to the period look of the interior. Ron and Nick had to make an exhaustive search to find just the right color green carpet.

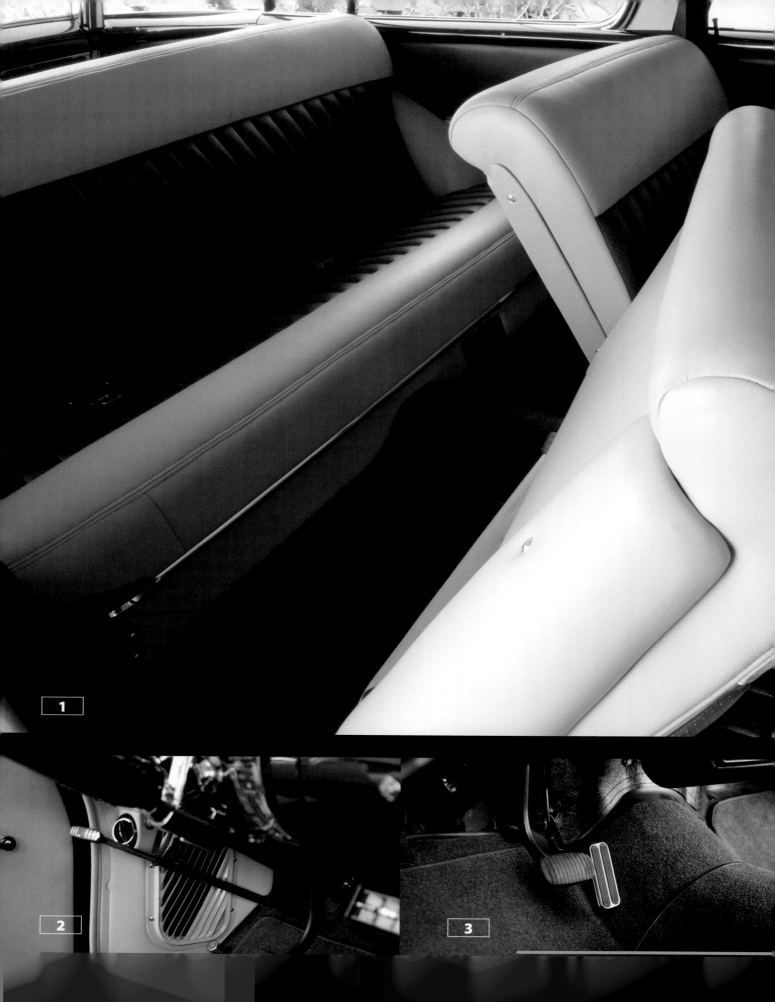

1
The folding rear bench seat was carried over from the original and trimmed in leather to match the front. Notice the six-disc CD changer under the rear seat on the driver's side. French stitching is used on the edges of the seats.

2
The vent grille in the kick panel was painted to match the surrounding leather.

3
Ron custom fabricated the carpet and mats.

4
Custom housings covered in leather were fabricated for the outboard air conditioning vents.

5
Ron used perforated green leather in both the door and rear quarter panels as well as the pleats on the seats. Rear speaker grilles are positioned in the lower rear quarter panels.

1

Nick's '55 Nomad is all ready for cruise night with room for six.

2

Perforated green leather is used above the stock stainless trim. Speaker grilles are painted to match, and are positioned just above the stock stainless trim.

3

The rear seat shows the way the stock seat curves around the rear wheel wells.

4

Ron sculpted the armrests, taking care to control the lower sweeping intersection to the lower part of the door panel. The armrests look original nested against the stock stainless trim, but the factory never built one like this.

5–6

Nick kept the stock instrument cluster, trim, and steering wheel.

7–8

The rear compartment is nicely trimmed in matching materials with an upgraded stock appearance.

1

5

6

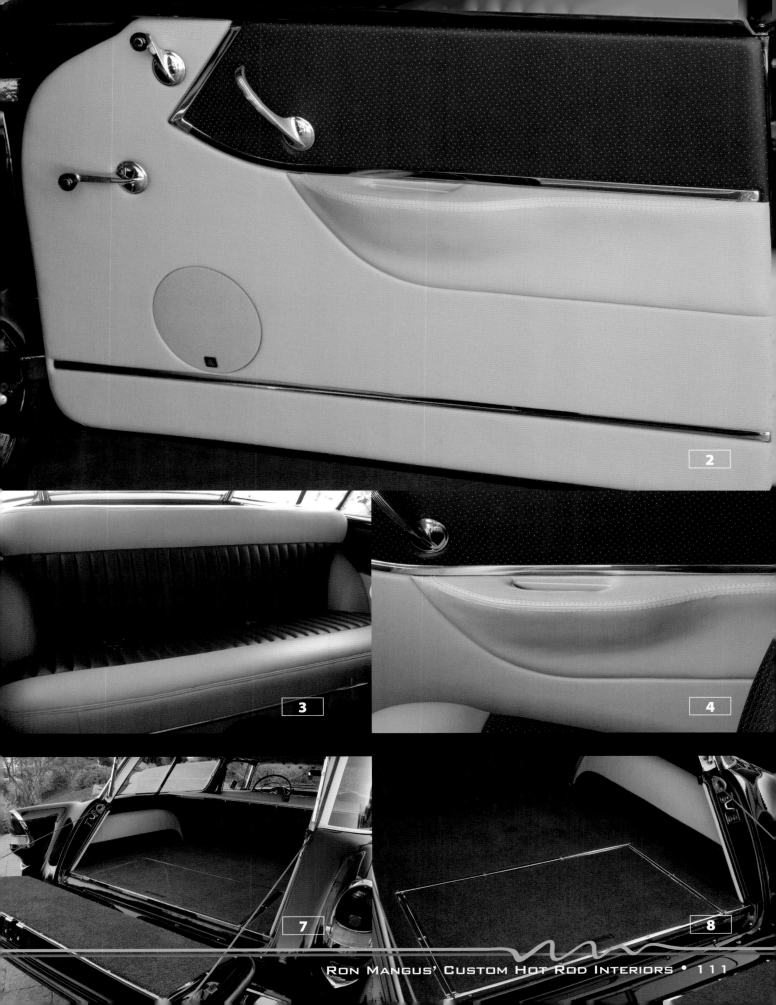

2

3

4

7

8

MIKE CAMPBELL'S
'57 Chevy Two-Ten

Mike stopped at a 7-Eleven convenience store in Arlington, Texas, and there was this faded black '57 Two-Ten sitting there. This technique of acquiring cars usually never works, but Mike waited for the car's young owner, and asked if he'd like to sell it. As a matter of fact, the owner could use some cash to fix up his '64 Impala. A deal was struck, the car parked, Mike drove the young man home, and mailed him a check the next day.

The car had badly faded black paint that just couldn't be brought back. So Billy Ratliff and David Horner of Restoration Specialties took it upon themselves to strip the car and repaint it while Mike and his wife Marilynn were on a trip. They obviously have a good relationship with Billy and David.

After the car was painted, the bone stock interior just wasn't cutting it. They were looking at Ron's website, and Marilynn asked why they couldn't have an interior like that in their car. They contacted Ron, flew to California, and met him for the first time at the Grand National Roadster Show in Pomona in January. The interior and the car was finished in April 2008. Ron's interior captures the flavor of the original by retaining the stock stainless door trim and extensively reworking the original seats.

The car has that '50s sleeper look about it, kicked high in the rear with big tires in the back, and not much chrome trim. The interior is completely upgraded and comfortable, but retains the essence of the factory design. Mike and Marilynn couldn't be happier with the way the car turned out.

Build and Paint: Restoration Specialties, Marble Falls, Texas
Engine: Paul Pfaff 540, Huntington Beach, California
Drivetrain: Turbo 400, Ford 9-inch rear end
Chassis: Modified stock
Wheels: 15" steel Rallyes

The instrument panel, package tray, and all of the interior window trim is black, tying all of those elements together visually, and thinning the appearance of the interior. Ron extensively reworked the stock seats adding much needed lumbar support, thigh and side bolsters to help hold the occupants in the seats. The stock radio is just for looks. It's not hooked up and probably never will be. Mike doesn't listen to the radio.

Ron kept the stock stainless door and rear quarter panel trim, but sculpted custom armrests, updating the interior styling considerably.

1

The space between the seating areas in the back seat provides side support and duplicates the front seat design. French stitching, very controlled with conservative shapes and curves, contributes to the "stock sleeper" look of the car.

2

Stock handles were retained. Notice the smooth and perforated leathers used together throughout the interior. The use of different material textures makes for a much more interesting interior.

3

The back of the stock seat is upholstered in matching smooth leather. With just a quick glance you wouldn't realize it's not stock.

4

The armrest on the rear quarter panel carries the design line started on the doors. The armrests have smoothly sculpted forms that blend outward and down to the stock stainless trim.

5

The rear seat and rear quarter panel sit comfortably together. The understated forms help carry the period theme of the entire interior.

1

2

3

4

5

1

Stock seats were completely reworked in Ron's shop. Front of seat has a waterfall design, where the thigh bolster ends the side bolster form, and the stitching and leather continues to the floor.

2

Door panels have a carpeted strip along the bottom edge for visual interest and to protect the lower door from scuffing.

3

The perforated and smooth leathers together create pleasing visual interest.

4

The headliner is covered in a fabric called Dynasty, which GM used in the '90s for seats.

5–6

The rear wheel wells are tubbed. Ron designed removable covers that go all the way back to the trunk opening, and hide storage areas for the battery and anything else you might want to keep with the car. Notice the fit and finish, carpeted edging, and the interesting leather covered close-out panel under the rear window. There are also leather strips in the deck lid hinges.

7

Underside of the deck lid is covered in the same cloth material as the headliner.

8

The kick panels have the same carpet strip continued from the doors.

1

5

6

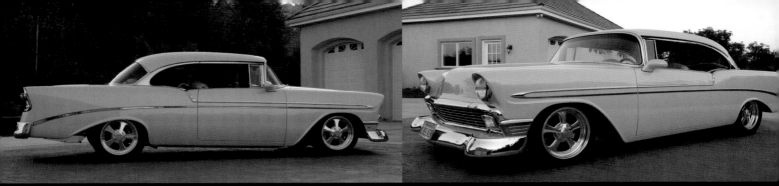

GEORGE JOHNSON'S
'56 Chevy Bel Air

When George found this rust-free classic it was owned by a friend of a friend and had been sitting outside under a tarp for years in southern California. The car was in basically pretty good condition. It took two years to complete, and was finished in June 2006.

The LS1 Corvette-powered yellow pearl show stopper has an interior with the look and feel of a contemporary luxury touring car. The instrument panel was completely restyled, and an instrument cluster from a 2001 Camaro installed. The chassis has Corvette independent suspension front and rear, and the suspension, driveshaft, and fuel tank are all polished aluminum.

Ron and George discussed what George was after in the look and feel of the interior, and created a personal luxury car inside this '56 Chevy Bel Air. The owner selected donor front and rear seats from a 1996 Cadillac Eldorado because they fit the bill in terms of the style and comfort he was looking for. The floor of the car had to be extensively modified and braced to accommodate the Eldorado front seats.

The interior features French stitching, sculpted door panels and headliner, and a custom center console. The light saddle leather with the yellow pearl exterior shouts southern California.

Build and Paint: Fred's Custom Wiring, Ontario, California
Engine: Chevy LS1
Drivetrain: GM 4L60E transmission
Chassis: Custom fabricated by Don Butler using Corvette
        independent suspension
Wheels: 16" Billet Specialties Legacy

1996 Cadillac Eldorado seats were re-sculpted and finished in light saddle leather and set the tone for the entire interior.

The thoroughly modern design of this interior completely disguises the car's true age. Its theme and custom features convey contemporary luxury, comfort, and style in every respect.

1
Ron modified the plush 1996 Eldorado rear seat to fit the '56 Chevy. The sculpted rear armrests carry the door design theme onto the quarter panels, and the custom map pockets on the backs of the front seats. The front shoulder belt retractors are hidden in the rear quarter panels, and are exposed through an opening with a chrome bezel.

2
Custom speaker grilles are painted to match the leather.

3–4
The highly modified instrument panel houses a 1998 Camaro instrument cluster, and the console shifter came from the same car. The dash modifications were fabricated by Mike Kilger, San Bernardino, California.

5
The sculpted kick panels add a custom touch, and make a great backdrop for the under-dash lighting. Every interior panel is carefully thought out.

2

3

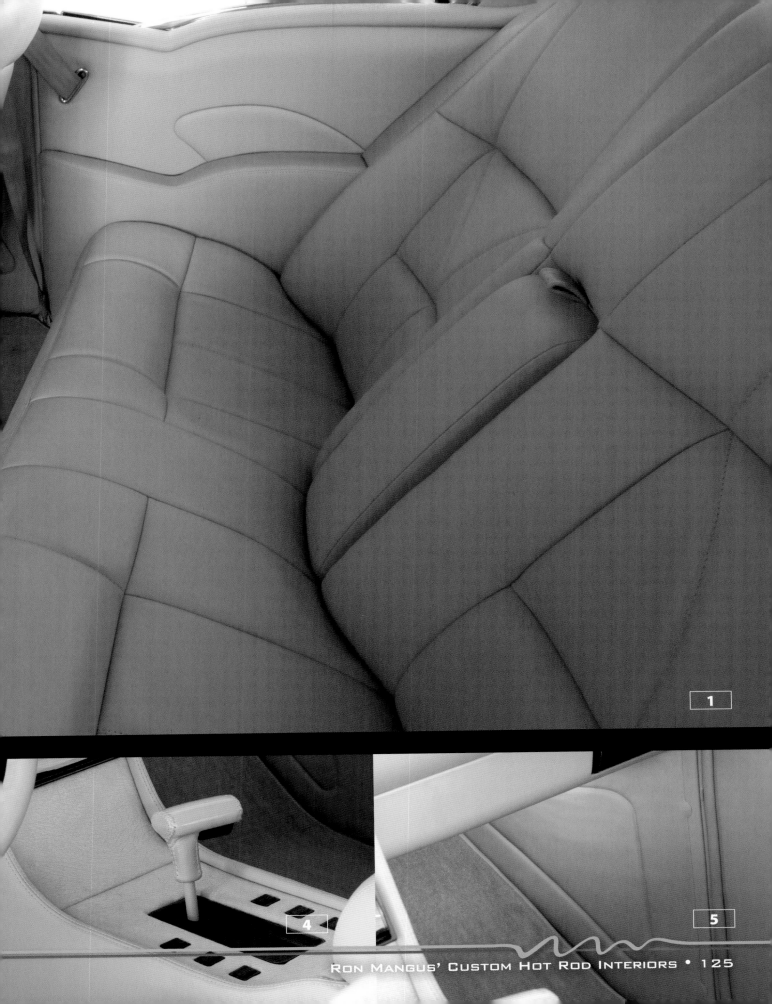

1

4

5

1

The Cadillac Eldorado front seats provide a great solution for adapting shoulder straps to this Bel Air hardtop.

2

The highly stylized sculpted door panels complement the seat design, and make a strong styling statement of their own. Notice the speaker placement used as graphic element, and the use of the late-model door handle.

3

Air conditioning controls are hidden behind this flip down panel in the console.

4

The console cover houses a convenient pull-out cup holder.

5–6

There is plenty of room in the rear quarter panel to conceal battery jumper posts and the fuse box. The shape of the storage cover repeats the interior theme.

7

The deck lid has a full fiberglass cover that matches the headliner in color and shape.

8

The stereo amps are mounted in this cool alcove under the package shelf. Notice the arch-shaped upper valence.

1

5

6

DON REDDING'S
'55 Chevy Two-Ten

When Don bought this '55 in 2002, he took the baby blue and white car to Billet Works Performance to have air conditioning and power steering installed, and one thing led to another. They ended up taking every nut and bolt out of the car, and four years later transformed it into this. The car was completed in July 2006.

This beast has a 750 hp, 540 cubic inch full-roller Merlin, and because Don didn't want to cut a hole in the hood, a Kinlser cross-ram EFI was installed, the third one made. Gear Vendor built Turbo 400 and 9-inch Mark Williams third member and axles harness the power. Yet the car is smooth going down the road and a pleasure to drive.

Ron Mangus designed the interior, using cut-down Lexus front seats, and designing the rear seat to match. Ron worked around the painted roll cage to design and install the interior. Especially challenging were the tight clearances between the roll cage and the headliner. Gray leather complements the pewter and bronze metallic exterior. The inviting, tailored interior disguises the potentially brutal nature of the car. We would classify this '55 in the far end of the luxury-performance category.

The Chevy's other features include custom made stainless steel fuel lines, stainless-steel steering column, serpentine drive system, 20-gallon fuel cell, four-wheel disc brakes by Aerospace Components, and a custom exhaust system with 5.5" collectors.

Built by: Billet Works Performance, Canyon Country, California
Paint: Joe Martinez
Engine: 750 hp, 540 CID full-roller Merlin
Drivetrain: Gear Vendor built Turbo 400, Mark Williams third
    member and axles
Wheels: 15" American Racing Torq-Thrust II
Tires: front: Goodyear, rear: Hoosier

Don's car is an interesting marriage of outrageous performance and supple luxury—between hard metallic painted metal and glove soft leather.

Cut down Lexus seats trimmed in smooth and perforated leather in the seating areas form the basis for the luxury part of this luxury-performance hot rod.

1
Climbing around the roll cage into the back seat may be a challenge, but once settled in, you'd be comfortable. Gray German square-weave carpet and mats protect the floor.

2
Racing shifter with line-lock betrays the purposeful nature of the car.

3
The dash is trimmed in bright billet and stainless.

4
The all-metal console has cupholders, storage, and houses large speakers decorated with custom chrome trim.

5
Kick panels with their large speakers are trimmed in perforated gray leather.

4

5

There is no room for sun visors, so no sculpted pockets. The windshield tinting will have to suffice. The large tach reminds the driver that this machine is all business.

2
On the door panels, lower design lines flow with the roll cage angles. The armrest forms are designed to clear the cage as well. Notice carpet used as a design element on the lower part of the doors.

Package shelf trim has sculpted speaker recesses.

4
Ron pays attention to every detail, right down to the shapes of the floor mats.

5
The instrument panel blends the colors and textures of the hard, polished trim and painted surfaces.

6
Ron had to work around the roll cage to fabricate and install the ultrasuede® headliner.

7–8
The design of the trunk trim continues the interior theme. Fit and finish are superb. The wheel well intrusions into the trunk are necessary to clear the tubbed body required for tire clearance.

1

5

6

2

3

4

7

8

RUSS SMITH'S
'56 Chevy Bel Air Nomad

It's difficult to believe by looking at the photos, but this stunning example of a Tri-Five Nomad started as a complete basket case, needing body work on all panels, all of the chrome redone, and stainless straightened. Russ purchased the car at the car corral event at the San Diego Good Guys car show.

Russ started with the name "Lomad" in mind, and designed the car to match the description. The car is built as a driver and handles like a sports car thanks to the Art Morrison Racing Chassis. The "Lomad" was built from the ground up in 16 months by Hot Rod Heaven, and was completed in October 2005.

Ron Mangus designed the interior theme, starting with Acura front seats to set the tone and style of the interior. His fully-integrated design breaks from tradition—the interior has a fresh, custom-contemporary, factory-like styling, with a few hot rod touches to spice things up. Ron used soft dove gray leather for the seating and door panels, artfully combining the hard look with pleated accents. The headliner is red ultrasuede® leather.

Other unique interior design elements include a Pioneer touch screen DVD, and a unique rear-facing DVD player for tailgate parties. Serious sound is provided by a 1,000 watt Kicker amp system with six speakers and subwoofer.

Built by: Hot Rod Heaven, Murrieta, California
Paint: 1999 GM Wildfire Red by Dick Jimenez, Hot Rod Heaven
Engine: Chevy LS1
Drivetrain: 700R4 transmission, Ford 9-inch rear end.
Chassis: Art Morrison, Fife, Washington
Wheels: 18" Boyd Coddington Stingray
Tires: BF Goodrich G-Force T/As

The styling contours, side bolsters, and lumbar support of the Acura front seats contribute to the luxury sports car feel of the interior.

This design fully integrates a flowing theme that runs through the car, creating a high-end look. Subtle material texture differences add to the sophisticated feel by combining a "hard-look" with perforated and pleated dove gray leathers.

1
Ron fabricated individual rear seating to match the front seats, maximized for comfort with good lumbar and side bolster support. Notice the pockets built into the backs of the front seats, and the quality of the lines and stitching throughout. Nomads didn't come with rear armrests, but the ones designed for this car carry the design theme that begins at the front doors and carries into the rear quarters. The rear seat is fixed, and the individual buckets contribute to the sports-luxury feel of the interior.

2
The rear of the console is angled to provide additional room for passengers, and air conditioning ducts were added to increase rear passenger compartment ventilation.

3
The door panels repeat the seat design with pleated leather.

4–5
The console houses the six disc CD changer and power plug. The cover has European cabinet hinges.

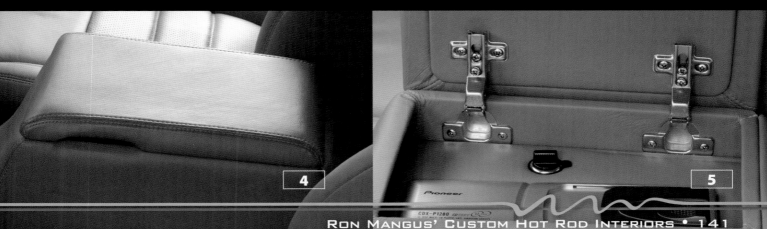

4

5

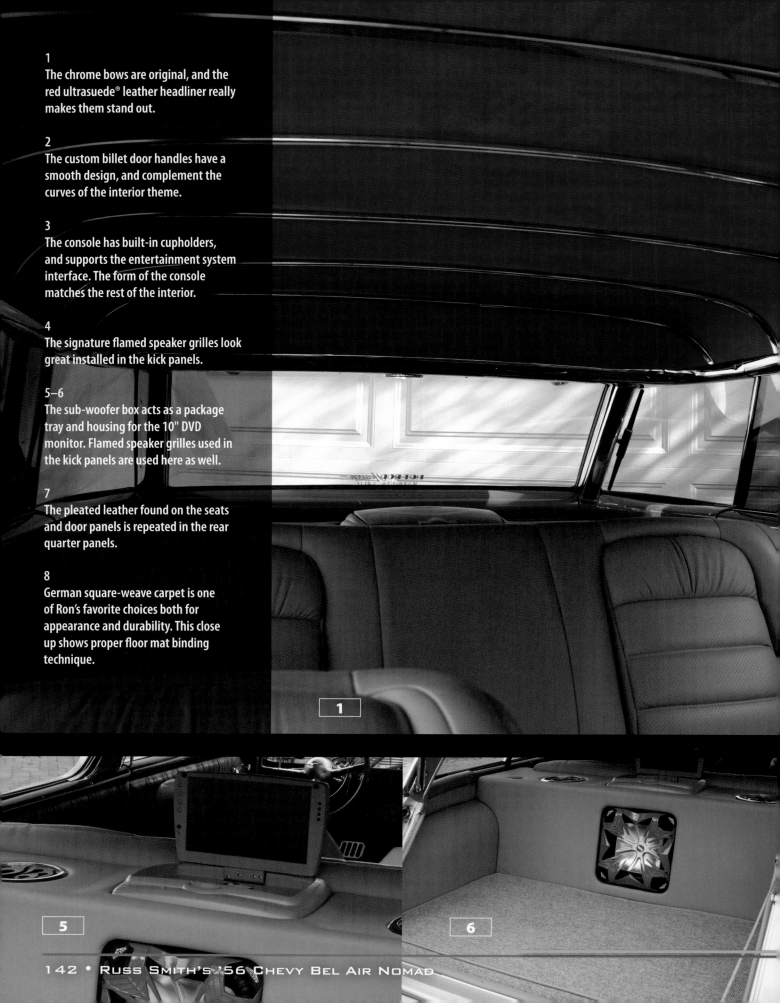

1

The chrome bows are original, and the red ultrasuede® leather headliner really makes them stand out.

2

The custom billet door handles have a smooth design, and complement the curves of the interior theme.

3

The console has built-in cupholders, and supports the entertainment system interface. The form of the console matches the rest of the interior.

4

The signature flamed speaker grilles look great installed in the kick panels.

5–6

The sub-woofer box acts as a package tray and housing for the 10" DVD monitor. Flamed speaker grilles used in the kick panels are used here as well.

7

The pleated leather found on the seats and door panels is repeated in the rear quarter panels.

8

German square-weave carpet is one of Ron's favorite choices both for appearance and durability. This close up shows proper floor mat binding technique.

1

5

6

2

3

4

7

8

'56 Chevy Bel Air

Chuck found this really nice '56 Bel Air hardtop in Anaheim in 2000. Nice as it was, Chuck wanted to tweak the car a bit, so he took it to Walton Fabrication in Upland, California. He was after a pro-street look. "Just tub the rear wheel wells and modify the chassis to make room for more rubber." Then came smoothing the firewall, and modifying the floor pan to accommodate Lexus 400 front seats. The modifications weren't really planned—it's just that one thing led to another. At this writing more is being done to the car. The headers are the lowest point of the car. Too low. Bag the front end? That would involve tearing up the interior to route air lines. Nobody wanted to do that. So they're changing the headers instead. When will the car be finished? Chuck's response: "Never."

Allen Edwards of Al's Body Craft put the finishing touches on the body. Al removed the hood bird, and Frenched the license plate adding a pencil-thin third brake light above the plate.

Ron's interior captures the spirit of what Chuck envisioned. Chuck had a great deal of welcomed input in the design process, and usually followed Ron's suggestions in regards to design and color selections. The interior is fluid and organic. The darker pigskin leather inlay that extends the full length of the instrument panel carries through to the doors, rear quarter panels, and continues in the trunk all the way to the back of the car. The Chevy "V" three dimensional relief in the trunk was Chuck's idea.

Built by: Walton Fabrication, Upland, California, and
Fred's Custom Wiring, Ontario, California
Paint: Allen Edwards of Al's Body Craft, Riverside, California
Engine: 502 Ram Jet by Street & Performance, Mena, Arkansas
Drivetrain: Gear Vendor transmission, Ford 9-inch rear end
Chassis: Modified stock
Wheels: Boyd Coddington Smoothie II, front: 17"×7", rear: 17"×13"

The stock instrument cluster housing is about the only clue as to what kind of car this interior is in. Note the leather insert in the instrument panel, and the sweeping curves in the lower dash and console.

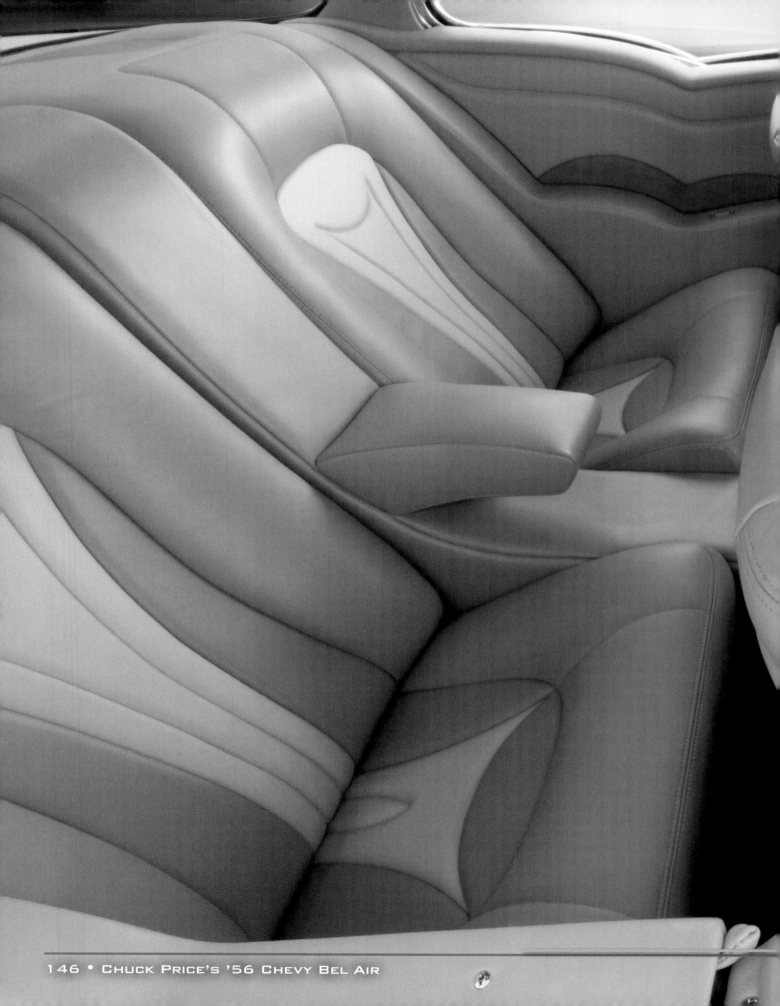

Ron had fun with this interior design. It features very fluid and organic styling, yet all of the shapes and curves resolve nicely. The upswept rear console and wild cantilevered center armrest make a bold statement.

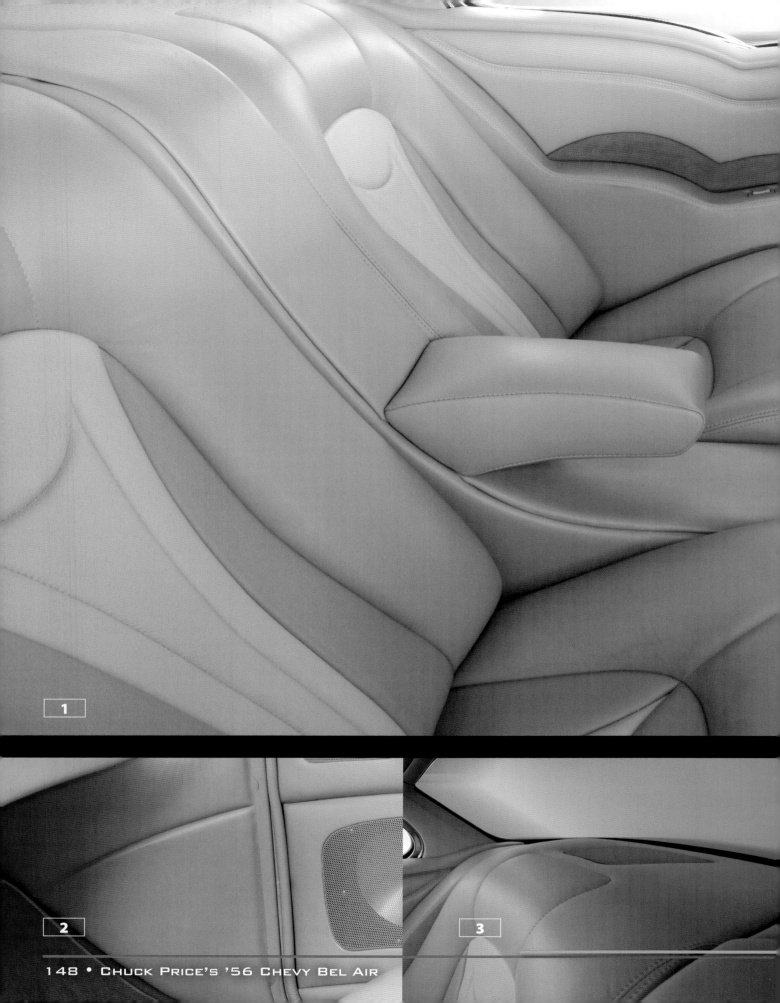

1

2

3

1
The Lexus front seats' contours are repeated in the back seats. The unique quarter panel armrests have a whimsical shape with contrasting leather inserts. The four bucket seat interior is dramatically divided by a wild upswept center console, and the rear headrests sweep up into the package shelf.

2
The sculpted design contour that runs through the doors begins on the kick panels.

3
The upper seat backs and the console wrap over onto the top of the package shelf, where there are more custom shaped speaker grilles.

4
The shape of the center stack echoes similar shapes found in the interior.

5
The entire interior is completely trimmed and finished with no unresolved areas. The lower dash close-out panels incorporate air conditioning vents and hide the plumbing. The lower curve of the panel is repeated in the trunk.

4

5

1

The cantilevered center rear armrest is readily apparent in this photo. The not-so-obvious areas like the close-out panel under the seat, oval courtesy light, and the fit and alignment of the lower console, carpet and mat have the same attention to detail as the rest of the interior.

2

Not much restraint shown in the door panel design. Wild, organic, and fluid. Speaker shapes add texture and interest. The curves are tightly controlled and the shapes complement each other.

3–4

The headliner did not escape the same unrestrained styling of the rest of the interior with its sculpted inset and contrasting leather accents. The headliner has smoothly shaped pockets for the sun visors.

5–6

The '56 is tubbed, and Ron covered the wheel well covers with the same vocabulary of forms started inside the car. One-piece amp cover is easily removed, and sculpted to match the theme of the car's interior.

7

Fiberglass deck lid cover is also sculpted to match and is leather wrapped.

8

The close-out panel under the rear window trimmed with the Chevy "V" was Ron's idea, but making it three dimensional was Chuck's.

1

5

6

2

3

4

7

8

'56 Chevy Bel Air Convertible

Janice's literal "dream" car, christened "Her 1956," ended its first life as a rust bucket, and was literally raised from ashes like the Phoenix. That's why there is a Phoenix bird on the hood. The car was completed in January 2008.

The car is bristling with custom and mechanical features, including a blown 502 big-block, which doubles as the car's only sound system.

True Fire™ flames are by Mike Lavallee of Killer Paint. He created the Phoenix on the hood, the flames on the side, and a portrait of Janice on the deck lid. The grille is from a 1951 DeSoto. This car is *personalized*.

Ron's interior is "over-the-top." He started with BMW front seats, custom built the rear seats, and sculpted the interior with flowing, full forms. The form transitions on the center console are beautifully executed, and the black leather is accented with bright blue seat back inserts. The custom convertible top is enclosed by a custom fiberglass boot cover fabricated in Ron's shop, covered in the same material as the top. It fits perfectly.

"Her 1956" has already won numerous awards, including First in Class for Outstanding Interior at the 2008 Grand National Roadster show in Pomona, California.

Build and Paint: Extreme Automotive, Corona, California
Airbrush Artist: Mike Lavallee of Killer Paint, Inc.,
    Snohomish, Washington
Engine: Chevy 502 with 671 Billet blower
Drivetrain: GM Turbo 400 transmission, Currie Ford 9-inch rear end
Exhaust: 3" by Chad's Custom Headers & Exhaust
Wheels: Boyd Coddington Junk Yard Dog, front: 17", rear: 18"
Tires: Nitto

The design of the interior in this unique '56 Chevy convertible is wild, but very tightly controlled. The cut down BWM seats with pronounced lumbar and side bolsters, typical of sports touring cars, set the feel of the entire interior.

When the car was at Ron's shop, the Groesbecks would come by every day to see the progress. The day Ron finished the interior, Janice predicted that they would win the award for the best interior at the Grand National Roadster Show. That's a pretty tall order for a black interior, and Ron was skeptical. She again predicted the win the last day of the show, and that night the car did indeed win the award for the best interior.

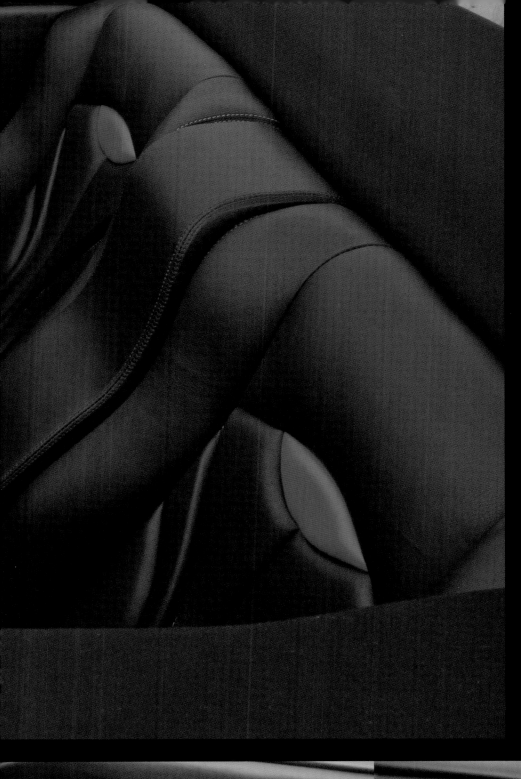

1
Undulating console surface parallels the seat's side bolsters, and complements the armrests. The rear seat shapes and contours are modeled after the BMW seats in the front.

2
The BMW seats were re-sculpted in "hard-look" black leather.

3
The lower door panel design swoops into the kick panel.

4
The door panels and armrests demonstrate restrained, tightly controlled design lines, allowing the console and sculpted seat design to have visual dominance.

5
Rear armrests blend into the convertible boot compartment with nicely swept forms. Very tight and controlled.

4

5

1

The front center console was built by Extreme Automotive, and supports a Ford F-150 Harley Davidson® Special Edition shifter with a hand-stitched leather cover.

2

The door panels are built-up with multiple pieces of 1-inch thick closed-cell foam. This construction process makes it possible to create an organic cross-section design with sweeping forms of tightly-controlled tapered shapes and highlights.

3

The design of the seats have an out-of-this-world, alien look. The bright blue leather inlays contribute to the effect.

4

The chrome instrument panel surrounded by the black leather really stands out. The massive console is the focal point of the interior.

5–6

The console's form is a beautiful sculpture on its own. Oval, chrome billet vents add visually to the alien look.

7

The hard convertible top boot snaps onto the car just like the factory's soft boot. Ron fabricated the boot from fiberglass, and covered it with the top material.

8

Upholstered in the same black leather, the trunk close-out panels are sculpted to complement the interior.

1

5

6

2

3

4

7

8

Thanks to our friends:

Acme Auto Headlining Co.
550 W. 16th St.
Long Beach, CA 90813
800-288-6078
www.acmeautoheadlining.com

Auto Custom Carpets, Inc..
P.O. Box 1350
1429 Noble St.
Anniston, AL 36202
800-352-8216
www.accmats.com

B & M Foam & Fabrics
3383 Durahart St.
Riverside, CA 92507
951-787-0221

Cerullo Performance Seating
2881 Metropolitan Place
Pomona, CA 91767
909-392-5561
www.cerullo.com

Extreme Automotive
18889 Grovewood Dr.
Corona, CA 92881
951-371-9730
www.extremeautomotive.org

Garrett Leather
(trade only)
1360 Niagara St.
Buffalo, NY 14213
800-342-7738
www.garrettleather.com

Glide Engineering, Inc.
10662 Pullman Ct.
Rancho Cucamonga, CA 91730
800-301-3334
www.glideeng.com

J & J Auto Fabrics, Inc.
247 S. Riverside Ave.
Rialto, CA 92376
909-874-3040
www.jjautofabrics.com

Keyston Bros.
(nationwide wholesale only)
1833 Riverview Dr., Ste. B
San Bernardino, CA 92408
909-796-5391
www.keystonbros.com

LeBaron Bonney
P.O. Box 6
6 Chestnut St.
Amesbury, MA 01913
800-221-5408
www.lebaronbonney.com

Original Parts Group
1770 Saturn Way
Seal Beach, CA 90740
800-243-8355
www.opgi.com

Quality Heat Shield
555 N. Main St.
Riverside, CA 92501
951-788-2903

Robbins Auto Tops
321 Todd Ct.
Oxnard, CA 93030
805-604-3200
www.robbinsautotopco.com

Ron Mangus Hot Rod Interiors
247 S. Olive Ave.
Rialto, CA 92376
909-877-9342
www.ronmangusinteriors.com

Tea's Design
2038 15th St. NW
Rochester, MN 55901
800-791-7328
www.teasdesign.com

The Truck Stop
dba Specialty Conversions
1889 W. Commonwealth Ave.
Fullerton, CA 92833
714-870-7920
www.buckle-up.net

Veteran Company
(wholesale only)
5060 W. Pico Blvd.
Los Angeles, CA 90019
800-524-3330
www.veteranco.com